ORIOLE PARK BRANCH

DATE DUE

1-04

SEP 0 2 2004		
OCT 0 8 2004		
MAY 2 4 2005		

DISCARD

DEMCO 38-296

DK EYEWITNESS BOOKS

FIRST LADIES

Written by
AMY PASTAN

In Association with the

Smithsonian
Institution

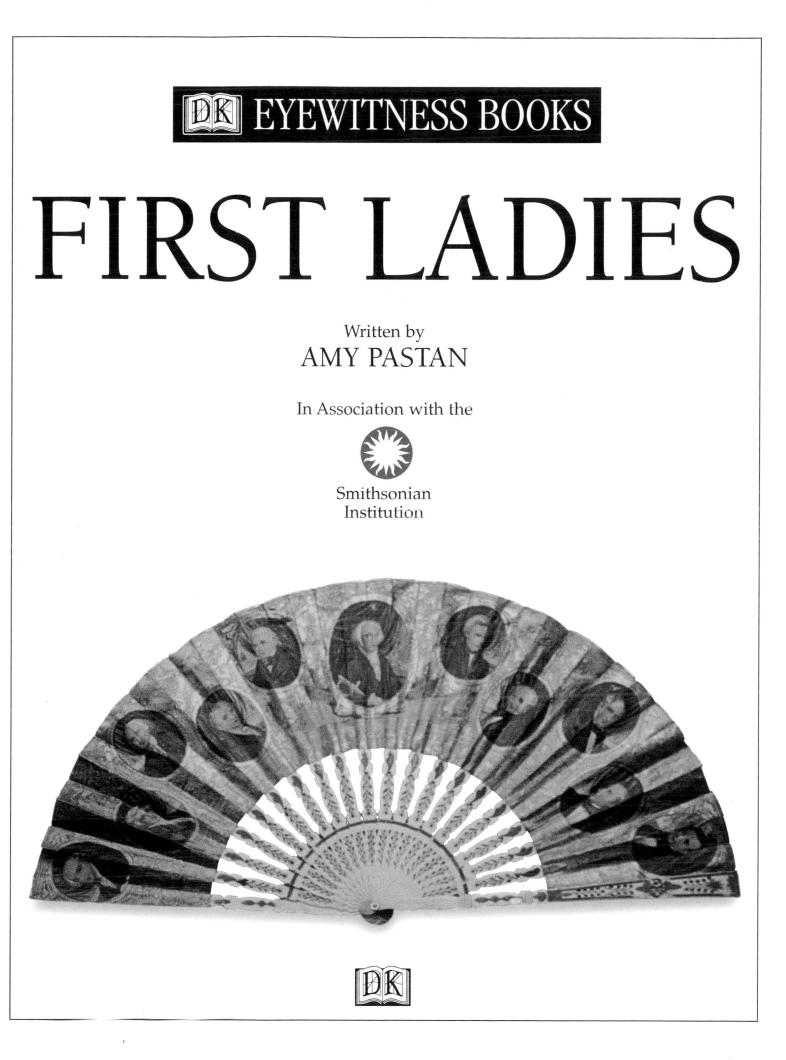

DK

DK

London, New York, Sydney, Delhi,
Paris, Munich, Johannesburg

Editor Andrea Curley
Designer Jane Horne
Senior Art Editor Michelle Baxter
Art Director Tina Vaughan
Publisher Andrew Berkhut
Production Director David Proffit

Jacqueline Kennedy's
Graflex camera

Mamie
Eisenhower
piggy bank

Frances Cleveland plate

Grace Coolidge's Native American bracelet

First American Edition, 2001
2 4 6 8 10 9 7 5 3 1
Published in the United States
by Dorling Kindersley Publishing, Inc.
95 Madison AvenueNew York, New York 10016

Dorling Kindersley Publishing, Inc. offers special discounts for bulk
purchases for sales promotions or premiums. Specific, large-quantity
needs can be met with special editions, including personalized
covers, excerpts of existing guides, and corporate imprints.
For more information, contact
Special Markets Department, Dorling Kindersley Publishing, Inc.,
95 Madison Avenue, New York, NY 10016 Fax: 800-600-9098.

Library of Congress Cataloging-in-Publication Data
Pastan, Amy.
        First ladies / by Amy Pastan.— 1st American ed.
                p. cm. — (Dorling Kindersley eyewitness books)
        Includes index
        ISBN 0-7894-7397-6 (hc) — ISBN 07894-7398-4 (lib. bdg.)
        1. Presidents' spouses—United States—Biography—Juvenile
literature. [1. First ladies. 2. Women—Biography.] I. Title. II. Series.
E176.2.P363 2001
973'.09'9—dc21
[B]   00-055541

Reproduced by Colourscan, Singapore
Printed in China by Toppan Printing Co. (Shenzhen) Ltd.

See our complete catalog at
www.dk.com

Abigail Adams's embroidered shoes

Hillary Rodham Clinton campaign butto

Martha Washington States china

Dolley
Madison's
silk robe

Martha Washington's trunk

Eleanor Roosevelt
postage stamp

Contents

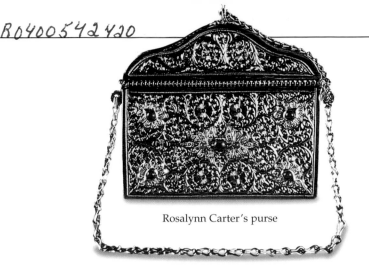

Rosalynn Carter's purse

Martha Washington

AMERICA'S INITIAL FIRST LADY was a simple and dignified woman who was more at home managing a country estate than fighting political battles. Martha grew up on a plantation in the British colony of Virginia. Her first husband died after eight years of marriage, leaving her with two small children and a large inheritance. During the Revolutionary War, which lasted from 1775 to 1783, she followed her second husband, General George Washington, from camp to camp, and was admired for her faithfulness and patriotism. Martha was already a grandmother when Washington became president of the new American democracy in 1789. The public called her Lady Washington. Although she would have preferred a more private life and perhaps a less noble title, Martha understood the importance of her role and set an admirable example for the women who followed her.

Martha was not fond of political life, but she respected her husband for "obeying the voice of his country."

Brocade fabric

SEWN WITH CARE
Martha Washington was known for her needlework. A note left by her granddaughter Eliza Parke Custis states that "this Quilt was entirely the work of my Grandmother as far as the plain borders. I finish'd it in 1815 & leave it to my Rosebud." Rosebud was Eliza's daughter Eliza L. Rogers. Martha kept her needles in this leather-and-brocade case.

A RELUCTANT CORRESPONDENT
Like most women of her time, Mrs. Washington had little formal education. She learned how to read and write so that when she married and moved away from home, she would be able to communicate with her family.

Revolutionary wives

Women played a large role in the American Revolution. Martha Washington's contribution during this historic period is especially well known because her husband served as commander in chief of the colonial army before becoming president. Risking her own safety, Martha traveled thousands of miles from the comfort and security of her home to visit General Washington at his various field headquarters. While at those camps, she tended the sick and saw to her husband's needs. Mrs. Washington was by no means the only wife whose devotion took her away from home during America's War of Independence. Many women followed their soldier-husbands. They washed and mended clothing, and cooked food. Some even took their spouse's place in battle if he was wounded.

Martha Washington's expense report

A DASHING SUITOR
The death of her first husband left Martha Custis a wealthy widow. Although she had many suitors, she was quickly impressed by George Washington, who had fought Indian wars in the West and was active in Virginia politics. After marrying him in 1759, Martha, with two-year-old Patsy and four-year-old Jacky, moved to his home at Mount Vernon in Virginia. Then she fulfilled the role of an eighteenth century wife by devoting herself to his career and managing their household.

AN ARMY WIFE
When Martha visited General Washington in the field, she probably would have seen him planning his battle strategies in this tent.

REPORTING A LADY'S TRAVELS
From 1775 to 1782, Martha weathered many harsh winters to see George, and he later reported her travel expenses. Her 1778 trip to Valley Forge, Pennsylvania, is noted here. It must have been a difficult visit, for the troops were suffering from intense cold, as well as the lack of shelter and food.

ON THE GO
Throughout the Revolutionary War, Martha packed and repacked her belongings in this sturdy trunk. Her trips to military sites up and down the east coast were long, uncomfortable, and dangerous. Not all colonists supported independence from Great Britain.

RELIEF EFFORTS
Mrs. Washington visited colonial forces camped at Newburgh on Hudson, New York, in 1782. Martha often contributed to the comfort and morale of the troops by mending uniforms and knitting warm wool garments. She spearheaded relief efforts for soldiers by organizing women of the colonies to raise funds and roll bandages. Later, as first lady, she was especially gracious to war veterans.

Hostess for the nation

After George Washington was elected president in 1789, the Washingtons moved to New York City, the first capital of the United States. Martha continued to oversee the household in their rented home on Broadway. Well aware that she and her husband were on public display, Mrs. Washington was careful not to behave like royalty. Guests were frequently invited to their home for dinner parties and receptions, as well as to "drawing rooms," which were more relaxed gatherings.

The President of the United States and Mrs. Washington, request the Pleasure of Company to Dine, on   next, at   o'Clock. 179   An answer is requested.

Dinner invitation

Design of flowers and insects

Bustle

SYMBOL OF AN UNBREAKABLE BOND
The most prized china owned by the first lady was given to her by a Dutch trader in 1796. The pattern shows each state—there were fifteen at the time—bound together by a strong chain. This set is now called the Martha Washington States china.

State names

SETTING AN ELEGANT TABLE
Entertaining was an important part of public life for the president and first lady. This bowl is part of a set of Chinese blue-and-white porcelain dishes that were often used for elaborate meals. Mrs. Washington considered herself an "old-fashioned Virginia house-keeper," but many guests commented on the Washingtons' refined hospitality.

EIGHTEENTH-CENTURY STYLE
Fashionable dresses of the 1780s had a flat front bodice, a full skirt, and a bustle in back. Mrs. Washington's elegant gown is made of silk and is hand-painted with floral bouquets and various types of insects, such as ants, beetles, and wasps—popular themes at the time.

Martha Washington's initials

Chain symbolizing the strength of the new nation

Eleanor Parke Custis

George Washington Parke Custis

Martha Dandridge Custis Washington

PRESIDENT
George Washington

YEARS AS FIRST LADY
1789–1797

BORN
June 2, 1731
New Kent County, Virginia

MARRIED
January 6, 1759
Kent County, Virginia

CHILDREN FROM FORMER MARRIAGE
John Parke Custis
Martha Parke Custis

DIED
Age 70
May 22, 1802
Mount Vernon, Virginia

VIEWING THE CAPITAL CITY
The Washingtons never lived in Washington, D.C., during George's years as president, although the site for the future federal city had been chosen. This artist's print shows Martha pointing to a map of the planned capital while her grandchildren look at what the future holds for their country.

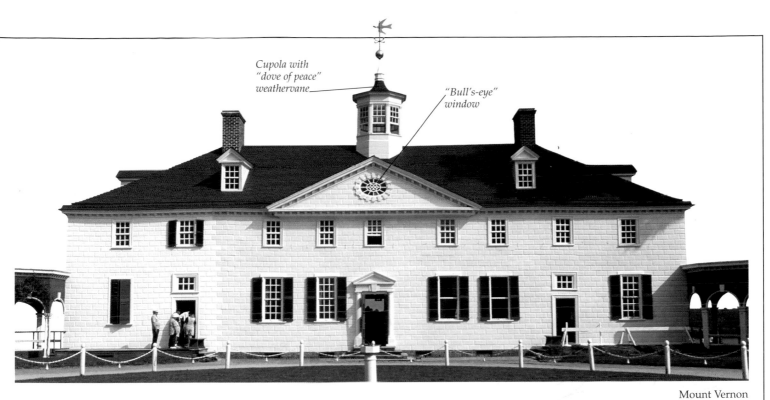

Cupola with "dove of peace" weathervane

"Bull's-eye" window

Mount Vernon

Home to Virginia

After George left the presidency in 1797, the Washingtons happily retired to Mount Vernon, their beloved home on the Potomac River in Virginia. Washington was just twenty years old when he acquired the plantation, and he eventually expanded the estate to eight thousand acres. A gentleman farmer, he rode twenty-five miles on horseback each day to inspect his fields. Meanwhile, Martha managed a busy household that received hundreds of visitors yearly. This may not have been the quiet withdrawal from public life for which the former first lady had hoped, but she graciously welcomed both invited guests and curious travelers who stopped for a glimpse of the man who had become a living legend.

Gilt-and-lacquered finish

Much of the fine furniture used by the Washingtons has survived to this day.

A TREASURED GIFT
The Count de Custine-Sarreck, who served with French forces in America during the Revolutionary War, gave George Washington a set of porcelain dinnerware. Martha used this pitcher at Mount Vernon and gave several pieces of the porcelain to friends and family members as mementos.

George Washington's initials in the center

AN UNBEARABLE LOSS
In 1799, George Washington developed a throat infection and died of it on December 14, at the age of sixty-seven. After his death, his wife retreated to an attic chamber on the third floor of their home. She could not bear to remain in their bedroom.

A FLAIR FOR STYLE
In the eighteenth century, it was usually men who dealt with the purchasing agents in Europe, so George may have ordered many specially designed pieces of furniture on Martha's behalf. She stored her jewelry in this dressing case.

Abigail Adams

ABIGAIL ADAMS HAS THE DISTINCTION of being the wife of one U.S. president and mother of another: John Quincy Adams. The strong-willed daughter of a New England minister, she was educated at home like most girls of her time. Her extraordinary intelligence, love of learning, and keen interest in politics made her the perfect partner for ambitious lawyer-turned-politician John Adams; and she is one of the few first ladies known for her own accomplishments rather than for her husband's. During the Revolutionary War, Mrs. Adams ran the family farm in Quincy, Massachusetts, as canon fire erupted not far from her doorstep. She was a true patriot who supported and influenced her husband, urging him to "remember the ladies." In fact, John's political rivals called the opinionated and outspoken Abigail Mrs. President, implying that she had too much political influence over him.

A HAPPY PARTNERSHIP
Although John Adams was proud, vain, and stubborn, his wife was his avid supporter during a marriage that lasted more than fifty years. When his popularity as president waned, Abigail never failed to defend her overweight husband against those who mocked the aristocratic style of His Rotundity.

Abigail, seen here at age fifty-six, spoke her mind and inspired future first ladies to take an active role in politics.

A TOKEN OF LOVE, AND SEPARATION
John Adams spent a good portion of his early career traveling both within and outside of the United States. In 1778, when he went to Paris to serve as the U.S. minister to France, he left Abigail behind. Before his departure, he gave his unhappy wife this locket.

Inscription reading "I yield whatever is, is right."

MY FRIEND . . .
More than two thousand letters written by Abigail Adams have been preserved. Eloquent, witty, and intelligent, they reflect on the great events of the Revolutionary War era and on the details of daily life for women in colonial times.

"My Friend" of the salutation is John Adams.

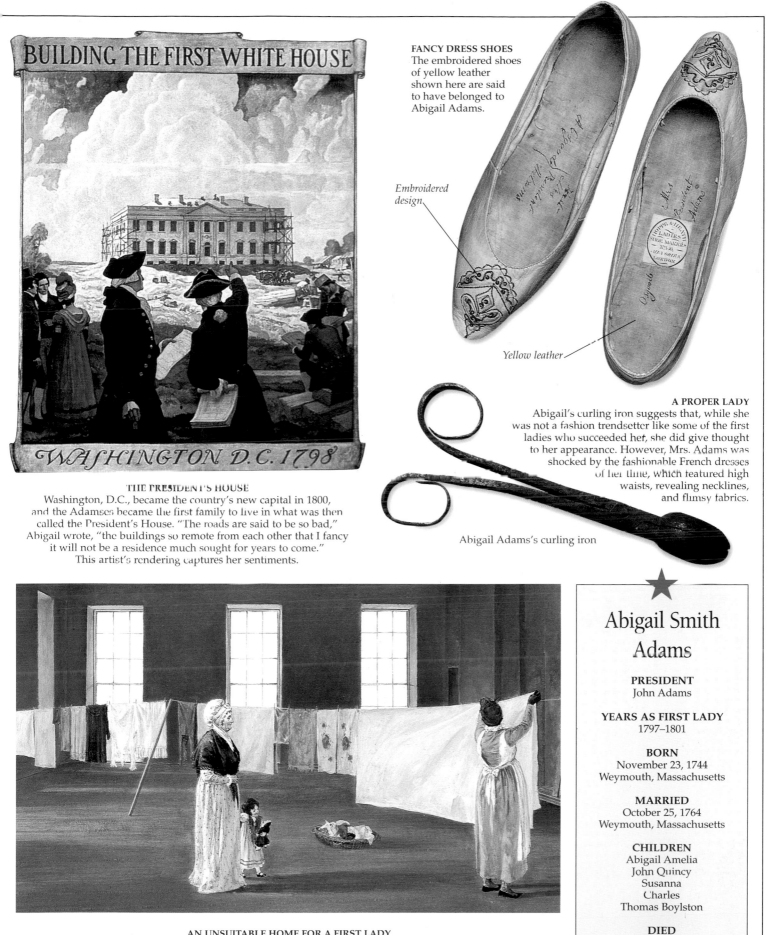

BUILDING THE FIRST WHITE HOUSE

WASHINGTON D.C. 1798

THE PRESIDENT'S HOUSE
Washington, D.C., became the country's new capital in 1800, and the Adamses became the first family to live in what was then called the President's House. "The roads are said to be so bad," Abigail wrote, "the buildings so remote from each other that I fancy it will not be a residence much sought for years to come." This artist's rendering captures her sentiments.

FANCY DRESS SHOES
The embroidered shoes of yellow leather shown here are said to have belonged to Abigail Adams.

Embroidered design

Yellow leather

A PROPER LADY
Abigail's curling iron suggests that, while she was not a fashion trendsetter like some of the first ladies who succeeded her, she did give thought to her appearance. However, Mrs. Adams was shocked by the fashionable French dresses of her time, which featured high waists, revealing necklines, and flimsy fabrics.

Abigail Adams's curling iron

AN UNSUITABLE HOME FOR A FIRST LADY
In 1966, artist Gordon Phillips painted this imaginary scene of the first lady coping with daily life in the unfinished Executive Mansion. This great room is now the elegant East Room. Mrs. Adams lamented, "We have not the least fence, yard, or other convenience . . . and the great unfinished audience-room I make a drying-room of, to hang up the clothes in."

Abigail Smith Adams

PRESIDENT
John Adams

YEARS AS FIRST LADY
1797–1801

BORN
November 23, 1744
Weymouth, Massachusetts

MARRIED
October 25, 1764
Weymouth, Massachusetts

CHILDREN
Abigail Amelia
John Quincy
Susanna
Charles
Thomas Boylston

DIED
Age 73
October 28, 1818
Quincy, Massachusetts

Martha Jefferson

Martha Wayles Skelton was a young widow of considerable wealth when she met, and married, a brilliant young Virginia lawyer named Thomas Jefferson. Though little is known about Martha and no portraits of her exist today, she and Jefferson shared a love of music and literature, and her husband later described his married life as "ten years of unchecked happiness." Sadly, the difficult births of six children took their toll on Martha. She died at age thirty-three—nineteen years before Jefferson was elected president in 1801. In the nineteenth century, it was considered improper for women to attend a social event if only men were present. Therefore, during his administration, Jefferson occasionally asked Dolley Madison (p. 12), a family friend and future first lady, as well as his oldest daughter, Martha Jefferson Randolph, to preside over official festivities. Future presidents who did not have a wife followed this practice, choosing a female friend or relative to serve as official hostess.

A GRIEVING HUSBAND
Thomas Jefferson won great fame as the author of the Declaration of Independence. He had expected to return to private life at Monticello, his Virginia estate, after serving his country at the Continental Congress in Philadelphia in 1776. However, the loss of Martha "wiped away all my plans and left me a blank which I had not the spirits to fill up." Jefferson's friends urged him to bury his grief and return to politics.

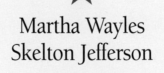

Martha Wayles Skelton Jefferson

PRESIDENT
Thomas Jefferson

YEARS AS FIRST LADY
Never served as first lady

BORN
October 30, 1748
Charles City County, Virginia

MARRIED
January 1, 1772
Charles City County, Virginia

CHILDREN
Martha
Maria
Lucy Elizabeth
Two girls and one boy
who died in infancy

DIED
Age 33
September 6, 1782
Charlottesville, Virginia

The top lifts to form a writing surface.

WRITING ABOUT LIBERTY
The mahogany lap desk on which Jefferson wrote the Declaration of Independence in 1776 was designed by him and built to his specifications by Philadelphia cabinetmaker Benjamin Randolph. Later, he gave this treasured object to his granddaughter Ellen as a wedding gift.

The drawer contains ink, quills, and other writing materials.

Unidentified young man

President Thomas Jefferson

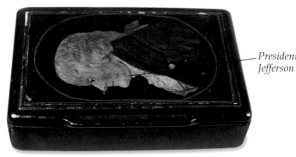

A POPULAR IMAGE
Portraits of presidents adorned objects during the eighteenth century, just as they do today. Jefferson's likeness is painted on the lid of this snuffbox. Snuff, a powder made of tobacco, was either inhaled or chewed. While men used snuff openly, it was generally considered inappropriate for women to do so.

THE PRESIDENT'S OFFICIAL HOSTESS

After the death of his wife, Thomas Jefferson came to rely on his oldest daughter, also named Martha. In 1784, she accompanied him to a diplomatic post in France, where she studied needlework, painting, history, reading, and Latin at a convent school. When Martha Jefferson Randolph sat for this portrait, she was fifty-one years old and the mother of eleven children.

The Jeffersons called this pitcher "the silver duck."

The obelisk, an ancient Egyptian architectural form, is a tapered column topped by a pyramid.

Martha Jefferson Randolph was nicknamed Patsy.

SKELTON SILVER

Martha Jefferson brought some possessions from her first marriage with her to Monticello. This elegant silver spoon was made in 1768 by Elizabeth Tookey of London.

Initials stand for Bathurst (Martha Jefferson's first husband) and Martha.

THE SILVER DUCK

The Jefferson family used this odd-shaped pitcher as a chocolate pot at Monticello. Its shape was based on a Roman pouring vessel known as an askos that had been excavated in Nîmes, France.

INVENTION AND AFFECTION

A man of incredible ingenuity, Jefferson designed this clock and had it crafted in Paris. The face rests between two obelisks. He chose this shape for his grave marker years later. After his death, Martha Randolph wanted this object because it had been so close to her father.

PLAYTIME AT MONTICELLO

When Jefferson's presidency ended, he returned to Monticello with Martha Randolph and her children. This rare view of Monticello, painted in Jefferson's lifetime, shows one of Martha's sons, George, rolling a hoop with a stick, a popular game at the time. Two of Martha's daughters, Mary and Cornelia, watch from the center of the garden.

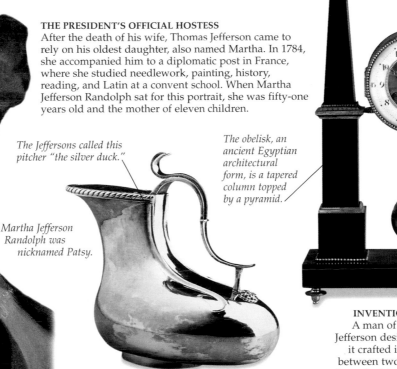

George Wythe Randolph

Mary and Cornelia Randolph

Dolley Madison

DOLLEY PAYNE TODD married Virginia congressman James Madison less than a year after her first husband, John, died in a yellow fever epidemic. By the time Madison was elected president, Dolley was an experienced and confident political wife. Although her well-known receptions—known as Mrs. Madison's Crush—were arranged to help advance her husband's career, the first lady never appeared to favor one guest over another—a skill that made her a powerful presence in the capital city.

A REVERED FIRST LADY
Mrs. Madison was so highly thought of that a seat was reserved for her in the House of Representatives, an honor never before granted to any American woman.

BY THE DAWN'S EARLY LIGHT
The British bombardment of Fort McHenry, in Baltimore Harbor, inspired Francis Scott Key to compose a song entitled "The Star-Spangled Banner." This later became the national anthem of the United States of America.

Saving the nation's heritage

When the capital of the United States was attacked during the War of 1812, first lady Dolley Madison rescued valuable state documents from the President's House just before British troops set fire to the mansion. This daring act, as well as her extraordinary charm, won her the everlasting admiration of the American public. Her husband did not fare as well. Having declared war on Great Britain for harassing U.S. ships, James was criticized for his inability to prevent British troops from invading American shores.

THE BRITISH ARE COMING
During the War of 1812, fourteen hundred British soldiers landed in Washington and began burning and looting the city. Dolley Madison kept her head in a crisis and was undaunted by having to relocate to temporary quarters. This painting is a modern artist's vision of that historic occasion.

A FIRST LADY RESCUES A GENERAL
Among the objects Dolley saved when fleeing the mansion on August 24, 1814, was this portrait of George Washington. She had her servants break the huge frame and roll up the canvas, which she carted away in the back of a wagon.

A capital hostess

Before Dolley Madison became first lady, she occasionally served as official hostess for Thomas Jefferson. Therefore, on entering the President's House, she was already respected as a leader of Washington society. Still, the first lady blossomed in her new role. At Madison's inaugural ball, the former Quaker, who had been raised to shun finery, looked like a queen, with an elaborate purple bonnet topped with white feathers. Her Wednesday evening receptions were open to all and became notable affairs. After James's death in 1836, she remained an important figure in the social circles of the nation's capital.

FATHER OF THE U.S. CONSTITUTION
The Madisons complemented each other perfectly. Dolley was outgoing and gracious. James was bookish and soft-spoken. A small and serious man, he brilliantly guided the writing of the U.S. Constitution and fought for a Bill of Rights.

★
Dolley Payne Todd Madison

PRESIDENT
James Madison

YEARS AS FIRST LADY
1809–1817

BORN
May 20, 1768
Guilford County, North Carolina

MARRIED
September 15, 1794
Harewood, Virginia

CHILDREN FROM FORMER MARRIAGE
Payne Todd

DIED
Age 81
July 12, 1849
Washington, D.C.

Embroidered design

Geometric designs

A DISH FOR DELIGHTFUL DESSERTS
This French porcelain was used for Dolley's dazzling state dinners at the Executive Mansion. She was the first to serve ice cream there.

SATIN SPLENDOR
Mrs. Madison wore this robe after she left the Executive Mansion. The style of the garment, with its raised waist, diamond-shaped back, and narrow sleeves that partially cover the hands, is fashionable for the 1820s. The silk satin is embroidered with butterflies, dragonflies, and phoenixes.

The incomparable Dolley Madison

Dolley had a warmth and vitality that drew people to her. In her later years, she served as matchmaker to President Martin Van Buren's son and offered expert advice to future White House residents. At her funeral in 1849, President Zachary Taylor declared, "She will never be forgotten because she was truly our first lady for a half-century." The term "first lady" stuck, and ultimately became the official title for the president's wife or official hostess. It was first used officially during Abraham Lincoln's administration.

A STYLE ALL HER OWN
In this portrait, Dolley wears one of her distinctive turbans. Her spectacular clothes invited ridicule, but most people felt, as one congressman's sister-in-law did, "there is something fascinating about her."

The lid is inscribed DPM.

JUST A PINCH
This silver snuffbox, made in England, belonged to Dolley Madison. Despite the fact that taking snuff was considered unladylike, the unique Dolley was known to indulge in this habit.

A GRACIOUS RETIREMENT HOME
After leaving the President's House, the Madisons retired to Montpelier, their Virginia estate. Dolley did not refrain from entertaining, however. Often there were so many guests for dinner that tables had to be set up outside.

Elizabeth Monroe

A QUIET FIRST LADY
Elizabeth Monroe absented herself from many White House occasions, perhaps because of poor health. Women of Washington society frowned on her behavior because social rules of the time prohibited them from attending official events if the first lady was not present. This disturbed the social and political networks in the nation's capital.

A SUBDUED SUCCESSOR to Dolley Madison (p. 12) as first lady, Elizabeth Monroe attended few formal functions, and many interpreted her reserve as being aloof and haughty. Despite her shyness, she played a key role in a diplomatic event while her husband, James, was serving as U.S. minister to France after the French Revolution. During that turbulent period, the French imprisoned and executed those who remained loyal to their former king. One suspected of such loyalty was the Marquis de Lafayette, a Frenchman who had helped Americans fight their own war for independence. Elizabeth dared to visit Madame de Lafayette when the noblewoman was imprisoned—and as a result, saved the patriot's wife from being beheaded.

A LEADER DURING GOOD TIMES
James Monroe was a popular president. During his tenure, the nation was experiencing a time of peace and tranquility, referred to as the Era of Good Feelings. However, little is known about his and Elizabeth's married life. The couple had two daughters. One of them, Maria, had the first White House wedding.

Lafayette's daughters   *Marquis de Lafayette*   *Madame de Lafayette*

A DARING RESCUE
The Marquis de Lafayette and his family were imprisoned in Paris because they were aristocrats. James Monroe felt that as an American diplomat he could not take any official action to help Madame de Lafayette, who was going to be put to death. Instead, James asked Elizabeth to drive to the prison to see her. News of the visit spread through the city and resulted in the noblewoman's release soon afterward.

THE "WHITE HOUSE"
During the War of 1812, the British had burned the Executive Mansion. By James Monroe's administration, the President's House was rebuilt and painted white. Thereafter it became popularly known as the White House. A native New Yorker, Elizabeth brought a European elegance to her new home—learned when she and James lived in France.

★

Elizabeth Kortright Monroe

PRESIDENT
James Monroe

YEARS AS FIRST LADY
1817–1825

BORN
June 30, 1768
New York, New York

MARRIED
February 16, 1786
New York, New York

CHILDREN
Eliza
Maria Hester

DIED
Age 62
September 23, 1830
Oak Hill, Virginia

Louisa Adams

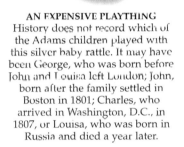

THE WIFE of John Quincy Adams disliked the demanding duties of first lady but rose to the task admirably. Born in England to a British mother and an American father, she discovered that the young diplomat she married was dour and inflexible. The disapproval of her mother-in-law, the formidable Abigail Adams (p. 8), made matters worse. Yet the European manners to which the senior Mrs. Adams objected made Louisa the most popular and successful hostess of her era in Washington. An accomplished musician, Louisa resented giving up her pleasures for John's career but felt she had no choice but to help her politically unpopular husband succeed at the expense of her personal happiness.

A PASSPORT TO ADVENTURE
When John became U.S. minister to Russia in 1809, Louisa gained entrance to St. Petersburg with this visa. When he was summoned to Paris after the War of 1812, Louisa and her young son Charlie made the dangerous forty-day trip across Europe in a Russian sleigh in the dead of winter.

AN EXPENSIVE PLAYTHING
History does not record which of the Adams children played with this silver baby rattle. It may have been George, who was born before John and Louisa left London; John, born after the family settled in Boston in 1801; Charles, who arrived in Washington, D.C., in 1807, or Louisa, who was born in Russia and died a year later.

A THWARTED MUSICIAN
Although she was a talented singer and harpist, Louisa had only one career option: to marry well and have children. She felt trapped in the White House, which she called "a dull and stately prison." Her journals reveal the frustrations of a woman whose abilities were not allowed to flourish.

UNPOPULAR PRESIDENT, DIFFICULT HUSBAND
John Quincy Adams was a scholarly man but also stubborn, serious, and negative. These qualities lost him a bid at reelection and made him a difficult husband as well. After his presidency, Adams served in the House of Representatives for many years. Louisa grew closer to him during that time, and won long-overdue respect for herself.

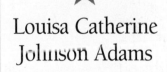

MUSIC IN THE WHITE HOUSE
Before moving into the White House, Mrs. Adams performed music for friends at social gatherings. She stopped when she became first lady at the request of her husband. Louisa did, however, host receptions at which other musicians performed.

John Quincy Adams had a distinguished career as a member of Congress.

★ Louisa Catherine Johnson Adams

PRESIDENT
John Quincy Adams

YEARS AS FIRST LADY
1825–1829

BORN
February 12, 1775
London, England

MARRIED
July 26, 1797
London, England

CHILDREN
George Washington
John
Charles Francis
Louisa Catherine

DIED
Age 77
May 15, 1852
Washington, D.C.

Rachel Jackson

RACHEL WAS BORN in Virginia and braved a dangerous journey through Cherokee territory at age twelve, when her family moved to Tennessee. At eighteen, she married Louis Robards. He showed himself to be a jealous, abusive husband who threw her out of the house three years after their marriage. In 1791, Rachel married Andrew Jackson, only to discover that her divorce from Robards was not final. While the matter was corrected in 1794, it surfaced again in 1828 when Jackson's political foes started rumors that Rachel was a bigamist—a person with more than one legal spouse—to discredit Andrew.

★

Rachel Donelson Robards Jackson

PRESIDENT
Andrew Jackson

YEARS AS FIRST LADY
Never served as first lady

BORN
June 15, 1767
Halifax County, Virginia

MARRIED
August 1, 1791
Natchez, Mississippi

Second ceremony
January 17, 1794
Nashville, Tennessee

CHILDREN
Andrew (adopted)

DIED
Age 61
December 22, 1828
Nashville, Tennessee

WRONGED RACHEL
The scandal about her marriage to Andrew took its toll on Rachel. In those days, being accused of bigamy was a vicious attack on a woman's morals. While Mrs. Jackson lived to see her husband win the presidency, she died of a heart attack only five days after the election.

MORE THAN JUST A HERO
Although raised in a log cabin, Andrew Jackson became a prosperous planter, a judge, and during the War of 1812, a military hero. A temperamental man, he nevertheless was a devoted husband who grieved deeply after Rachel's death.

TWO JACKSON HOSTESSES
The Jacksons had no children of their own. In 1809, they adopted a nephew and named him Andrew Jackson, Jr. Another nephew, Andrew Jackson Donelson, married Rachel's favorite niece, Emily. It was Emily whom the president asked to serve as hostess in the White House. A well-liked and tactful person, she died of tuberculosis in 1836. In the final months of Jackson's presidency, Sarah Yorke Jackson, the wife of Andrew, Jr., served as hostess.

Portrait of Emily Donelson, by Ralph E.W. Earl, a friend of Jackson

Portrait of Sarah Yorke Jackson, also by Ralph Earl

Sarah's guitar is made of spruce and rosewood, and is trimmed with ebony, ivory, and mother of pearl.

OPEN HOUSE AT THE WHITE HOUSE
During the presidential campaign, Jackson vowed to represent ordinary citizens. His inauguration day was marked by an open reception at the White House that became so unruly he had to flee. The enthusiastic public celebrating his victory practically vandalized the Executive Mansion.

Hannah Van Buren

HANNAH HOES and Martin Van Buren were cousins who grew up together in the Dutch community of Kinderhook, New York. Little is known about Hannah, who died of tuberculosis at age thirty-five. Van Buren never remarried; but soon after he took office in 1837, his eldest son, Abraham, married Angelica Singleton, who eventually served as her father-in-law's official hostess.

★
Hannah Hoes Van Buren

PRESIDENT
Martin Van Buren

YEARS AS FIRST LADY
Never served as first lady

BORN
March 8, 1783
Kinderhook, New York

DIED
Age 35
February 5, 1819
Albany, New York

A GENTLE WOMAN
The Van Burens' twelve-year marriage was believed to be a happy one. A niece remembered Hannah as having a "loving, gentle disposition."

AN ELEGANT PENDANT
Angelica Van Buren owned this pearl necklace with cut glass pendant. Her queenly manner was appreciated by some and despised by others.

Double strand of pearls

THE LITTLE MAGICIAN
Americans nicknamed Martin the Little Magician for his political tricks. The widower president moved into the White House with his four grown sons.

DOLLEY'S MATCH
When Dolley Madison (p. 12) introduced her cousin Angelica Singleton to Hannah and Martin's son, Abraham, they fell in love, and married in 1838.

Anna Harrison

ANNA HARRISON was the wife of one president and the grandmother of another: twenty-third president Benjamin Harrison. She married Revolutionary War officer William Henry Harrison on November 22, 1795, and they had ten children. William held various political offices before his election to the presidency in 1840. Due to the sudden death of one of their sons, Anna was not able to journey to Washington, D.C., for her husband's inauguration. One month after taking the oath of office, William Harrison became ill and died of pneumonia.

★
Anna Symmes Harrison

PRESIDENT
William Henry Harrison

YEARS AS FIRST LADY
March 4–April 4, 1841

BORN
July 25, 1775
Morristown, New Jersey

DIED
Age 88
February 25, 1864
North Bend, Ohio

A BRIEF FIRST LADY
Anna was still packing to make the long journey from Ohio to Washington, D.C., when she learned of her husband's untimely death.

THE HERO OF TIPPECANOE
In 1811, William Henry Harrison became a hero for his defeat of Chief Tecumseh at the Battle of Tippecanoe in the Indiana Territory.

LOG CABIN CAMPAIGN
The symbol of the log cabin was used during Harrison's run for the presidency in 1840 to identify William with the common man. This campaign item is from that election.

**A LITTLE-KNOWN
FIRST LADY**
As is the case with so
many women of the
nineteenth century, little
is recorded about Letitia
Christian's early life.

Letitia Tyler

LETITIA MARRIED JOHN TYLER just after he
was elected to the Virginia state legislature
and bore him nine children. Although a
stroke she suffered in 1839 left her partially
paralyzed, she moved to Washington after
John became vice president in 1841. When he
took over the presidency after William
Harrison's sudden death, Letitia found that
she had to yield the social duties of
first lady to her daughter-in-law
Patricia. Mrs. Tyler had a second
stroke on September 10, 1842, and
died in the White House partway
through John's presidential term.

Tyler campaign
banner

TYLER'S PLANTATION HOME
Sherwood Forest Plantation
was John Tyler's home
from 1842—the year of
his wife's death—to 1862.
Despite being damaged
by Union soldiers, it
survived the Civil War
intact, and continues
to be the home of
Harrison's descendants.

HIS ACCIDENCY
When William
Henry Harrison
died in office, Tyler
became the first vice
president to assume
the presidency without
being elected. This led
his critics to nickname
him His Accidency.

Julia Tyler

FOLLOWING Letitia's death, John soon
remarried. The second Mrs. Tyler was
a vivacious twenty-four year old who
became the talk of Washington. At
boarding school, Julia Gardiner had
sparked a scandal by modeling for an
advertisement. Her parents whisked
her away to Europe and then to
Washington, D.C., where she met,
and married, Tyler. She spent
only a few months as first
lady but delved into her
role with enthusiasm.

A PRO-SLAVERY PRESIDENT
John Tyler was an unpopular
president, partly due to his
support of slavery. His wife
shared his political views
and suffered for her
southern sympathies
during the
Civil War.

AN ENTERPRISING BRIDE
Julia Tyler adored her
role as first lady, and
held frequent dinner
parties and receptions.
After leaving the White
House, she signed some
of her letters "Mrs. Ex-
President Tyler."

**THE ROSE OF
LONG ISLAND**
The flirtatious Julia called
herself the Rose of Long
Island and may have
made the first celebrity
endorsement by modeling
for this advertisement.

Sarah Polk

SARAH TOOK ON A MORE independent role than was considered fitting for women of her era. The daughter of a rich Tennessee planter, she received a fine education but preferred politics to music and needlepoint. As first lady, she became known—and sometimes criticized-—for her opinions. Having once said that if her husband were elected president she would "neither keep house nor make butter," Sarah was good to her word. Perhaps because she had no children and few domestic responsibilities, she became James's adviser in private, read over his speeches, and worked with him as a partner on many aspects of state business. In public, however, she downplayed her role in Polk's administration.

Portrait of Sarah Polk done in 1846, by G.P.A. Healy

STRICT SARAH
Mrs. Polk's strict religious principles led her to prohibit Sunday receptions and dancing at the White House. Still, she proved to be a charming hostess and influential first lady.

★
Sarah Childress Polk

PRESIDENT
James K. Polk

YEARS AS FIRST LADY
1845–1849

BORN
September 4, 1803
Murfreesboro, Tennessee

MARRIED
January 1, 1824
Murfreesboro, Tennessee

DIED
Age 87
August 14, 1891
Nashville, Tennessee

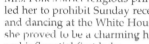

Banner from 1844 campaign

POLK AND DALLAS.

TEA AT THE WHITE HOUSE
This elegant blue-and-gold teapot, which is believed to have been used by the Polks at the Executive Mansion, was part of a set purchased in New York in 1845 for just eighty-five dollars.

POLK FOR PRESIDENT
Although he lacked the type of magnetism that generally attracts the public, James became the Democratic Party's presidential candidate in 1844, defeating the more personable Henry Clay.

George Washington
Andrew Jackson
Martin Van Buren
William Henry Harrison
John Tyler
James Polk
John Quincy Adams
James Monroe
James Madison
Thomas Jefferson
John Adams

THE POLK PARTNERSHIP
James Polk pledged to expand the land held by the United States to the Pacific Ocean. He accomplished his goal with the support of the first lady, who served unofficially as his personal adviser.

SARAH'S PRESIDENTIAL FAN
James gave his wife this fan to carry during the inauguration festivities in 1845. It shows images of all the U.S. presidents, up to and including Polk.

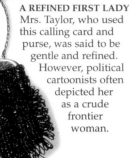

A REFINED FIRST LADY
Mrs. Taylor, who used this calling card and purse, was said to be gentle and refined. However, political cartoonists often depicted her as a crude frontier woman.

Beaded purse

Margaret Taylor

PEGGY SMITH grew up on a prosperous plantation in Maryland. After marrying Zachary Taylor in 1810, she spent the next fifteen years moving her family to remote military posts throughout the United States. At one point, she became seriously ill; and although she recovered, she was always treated as a semi-invalid. The Mexican War, which made her husband a general and a hero, ended in 1848. Mrs. Taylor looked forward to retiring with Zach to their Louisiana home. However, his election to the presidency later that year disrupted her plans. Peggy was so uncomfortable with her role as first lady that her daughter Betty Taylor Bliss served as official hostess.

OLD ROUGH AND READY
Zach Taylor was a professional soldier and earned the nickname Old Rough and Ready from the men he commanded. He had no political experience, but won the presidency due to his status as a war hero.

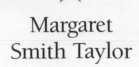

Margaret Smith Taylor

PRESIDENT
Zachary Taylor

YEARS AS FIRST LADY
1849–1850

BORN
September 21, 1788
Calvert County, Maryland

DIED
Age 63
August 18, 1852
Pascagoula, Mississippi

PERFECT BLISS
Mrs. Taylor never sat for a photograph. Her daughter Betty Bliss, pictured here, was only twenty-three when she took on the duties of running the White House. A lieutenant colonel's wife, Betty had great poise and charm.

Abigail Fillmore

ABIGAIL WAS THE *FIRST* FIRST LADY to hold a paying job before her marriage: she was a teacher for almost seven years during her twenties. In keeping with the custom of her time, she gave up her career after marrying Millard. By the time he became president in 1850 after Zachary Taylor's death, she was suffering from health problems.

Although her daughter took over as hostess, Mrs. Fillmore made a lasting contribution to future first families by creating a library in the White House.

A GREAT MIND
Abigail Fillmore was highly educated for a woman of her time, and had a thorough knowledge of the issues affecting her husband's administration.

Abigail Powers Fillmore

PRESIDENT
Millard Fillmore

YEARS AS FIRST LADY
1850–1853

BORN
March 13, 1798
Stillwater, New York

DIED
Age 55
March 30, 1853
Washington, D.C.

A HARDWORKING CHIEF EXECUTIVE
Millard Fillmore worked in a textile mill before embarking on a career in politics. His success in government is credited to hard work and a supportive wife.

Jane Pierce

Jane Appleton had a comfortable childhood in Brunswick, Maine. Her deeply religious parents opposed her engagement to Congressman Franklin Pierce because of his youthful drinking sprees, but the couple married in 1834 and moved to Washington, D.C. While Jane disliked politics so much that she had fainted when she heard Franklin had been nominated for the presidency, she delighted in her two infant sons.

LOVE AND LOSS
After her older son, Franklin, Jr., died of typhoid fever in 1844, Jane clung to her younger boy, pictured with her here. Benny's death in a train accident in 1852 sent her into crazed grief.

A SHADOW ON THE PRESIDENCY
Franklin Pierce was sworn in as the nation's fourteenth president shortly after eleven-year-old Benny died. In deep mourning, Pierce was not strong enough to prevent the country from coming closer to civil war.

NEVER-ENDING SORROW
Jane spent her years as first lady writing sad notes to Benny. She thought God had taken his life as punishment for Franklin's involvement in politics, which she thought to be "dirty."

Locket with a photograph of Benny inside

Harriet Lane

Harriet Lane was raised by her uncle James Buchanan. When the bachelor senator became president in 1857, twenty-six-year-old Harriet served as his official hostess. She brought glitter and glamour to an administration marked by growing hostility between the northern and southern states over the issue of slavery. After the Civil War, Harriet married Henry Elliot Johnston, a wealthy banker. Widowed eighteen year later, she devoted herself to worthy causes and donated her fine art collection—now at the Smithsonian Institution—to the nation.

A BACHELOR'S BEAUTY
Harriet was a flirtatious young woman with golden hair and violet eyes.

Prince of Wales

Harriet Lane

FIT FOR A PRINCE
In 1860, England's Prince of Wales made a historic visit with President Buchanan and Harriet Lane to Mount Vernon. Miss Lane invited the royal visitor to a series of White House receptions. She also challenged him to a bowling match —and won.

A DOOMED PRESIDENCY
The first bachelor to become the commander in chief, Buchanan was a dignified statesman. Still, he could not avoid blame for the Union's collapse.

Mary Lincoln

MARY LINCOLN had the misfortune to enter the White House as civil war divided the nation. Well-meaning and intelligent, her southern birth led northerners to suspect her of being a spy and southerners to condemn her Union sympathies. Her habit of spending a fortune on elegant clothes, which she believed were necessary for a first lady, was scorned by Americans who were suffering the hardships of war. Mary believed that slavery was wrong, but her efforts to speak out against it were misunderstood. Devoted to her husband and her position, she retreated briefly from public life when her eleven-year-old son Willie died in 1862. After Lincoln was assassinated in 1865, she was again plunged into grief, from which she never fully recovered.

The first lady's excessive spending on clothes and her redecorating of the Executive Mansion were her attempts to uphold the power and prestige of the presidency during its most serious national crisis.

OPPOSITES ATTRACT
In many ways, Abe and Mary were opposites. He was extremely tall and thin; she was short and rather plump. He had grown up in a log cabin in the backwoods of Kentucky; she had lived a comfortable, privileged life in the city. Despite their differences, their mutual interest in politics drew them together.

SCHOOLED ON THE FRONTIER
The name "Mary Lincoln" appears inside this copy of Thomas Buchanan Read's *Female Poets in America*. When she entered Washington society, the first lady was ridiculed as being an ignorant and unrefined frontier girl because she was from Kentucky. In truth, Mary had received an exceptional education and could discuss anything—from poetry to politics—with the elite members of the nation's capital.

THE FIRST FAMILY
Mary and Abe had four sons. However, only two—Robert, the oldest, and Thomas, nicknamed Tad, the youngest—lived past childhood. Eddie and Willie died young of illnesses that nineteenth-century doctors could not cure. Their loss took its emotional toll on Mrs. Lincoln, who became increasingly odd and unpredictable.

★

Mary Todd Lincoln

PRESIDENT
Abraham Lincoln

YEARS AS FIRST LADY
1861–1865

BORN
December 13, 1818
Lexington, Kentucky

MARRIED
November 4, 1842
Springfield, Illinois

CHILDREN
Robert Todd
Edward Baker
William Wallace
Thomas

DIED
Age 63
July 16, 1882
Springfield, Illinois

Black stripes

Off-white silk taffeta material

Purple flowers

FASHION AT ANY COST
In 1861, Mrs. Lincoln wore this two-piece gown for a photograph session with renowned photographer Mathew Brady. The extravagant first lady often shopped for fine fabrics in New York, and employed a full-time dressmaker, former slave Elizabeth Keckley, who became her close friend.

Game boards

Cards

Spinner

Chess pieces

Dice shaker

Dominoes

Checkers pieces

Dice

GROWING UP IN THE WHITE HOUSE
Born in 1853, Tad Lincoln was a little boy when his father became president. His elaborate game set unfolds to reveal a host of boards and playing pieces. Tad was only twelve years old when his father died. After the Lincoln family left the White House, his troubled mother came to depend on him for emotional support as if he were an adult.

Abraham Lincoln *Andrew Johnson* *Julia Grant* *Ulysses Grant*

Mary Lincoln

William Sherman

LINCOLN'S LAST RECEPTION
On the night of his second inauguration, President Lincoln held a special reception for the heroes of the Union cause. The guests included Major General Ulysses S. Grant and his wife, Julia, Vice President Andrew Johnson, and Major General William T. Sherman. This was the last formal event hosted by the first family. Lincoln was assassinated several weeks later.

23

Women and the War Between the States

Although President Lincoln believed that "a house divided cannot stand," he was unable to prevent the southern states from leaving the Union and forming the Confederate States of America. Civil war broke out shortly after his inauguration in 1861. Over the next four years, six hundred thousand American men lost their lives. Women's lives were dramatically affected by the conflict as well. With their husbands off to war, both northern and southern women took over important tasks outside the home. Many nursed the sick and wounded; others raised money for hospitals and military supplies while managing farms or plantations. Mary Lincoln frequently visited the suffering. Her compassion extended to African Americans. She was the first woman in the White House to invite black people to the Executive Mansion as guests. Famous abolitionist and ex-slave Frederick Douglass was among those who had tea with the Lincolns.

Women with soldier

Runaway slave Harriet Tubman. Slave owners offered a $40,000 reward for her capture, but she was never caught and the bounty money remained unclaimed.

A STRONG UNION
Throughout the war, Mary Lincoln supported her husband's political career. The success of the Union army bolstered the Lincoln-Johnson ticket during the presidential campaign of 1864. Lincoln was inaugurated for his second term on March 4, 1865. On April 9, 1865, Robert E. Lee, commander of the Confederate forces, surrendered to Union major general Ulysses S. Grant.

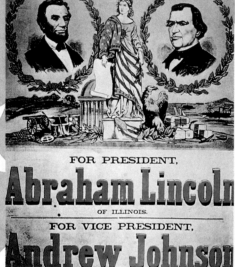

UNION NOMINATION
FOR PRESIDENT,
Abraham Lincoln
OF ILLINOIS.
FOR VICE PRESIDENT,
Andrew Johnson

Poster from 1864 campaign

AN ELEGANT PROTEST
Josiah Wedgwood, maker of the famous Wedgwood china, was an Englishman who opposed slavery. To further the abolitionist cause, he produced two ceramic images, one featuring a kneeling female slave and the other a male. These images were cast as tokens in the 1830s and were widely distributed by antislavery groups.

AM I NOT A WOMAN & A SISTER
1838

Bronze metal

UNITED IN A COMMON CAUSE
Mary Lincoln supported the abolitionist, or antislavery, movement. Many women who joined abolitionist groups realized they had something in common with those in bondage. They too were denied many basic rights, such as the right to vote. Harriet Tubman, pictured here, personally led hundreds of people to freedom on the Underground Railroad, the name given to a network of secret escape routes that took slaves north.

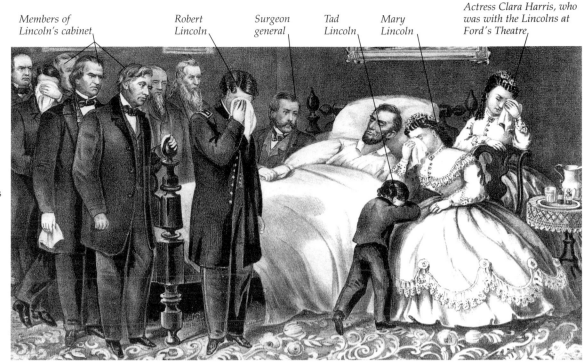

A PRESIDENT FOR THE AGES
On April 14, 1865, Abraham Lincoln was attending a performance of the play *Our American Cousin* at Ford's Theatre in Washington, D.C., when actor John Wilkes Booth entered the presidential box and shot Lincoln in the back of the head. The president was carried across the street to a boardinghouse. There he lay unconscious, surrounded by his family, his doctor, and cabinet members. He died the next morning. Following his death, a weeping secretary of war, Edwin M. Stanton, declared, "Now he belongs to the ages."

Buildings draped in black funeral bunting

Elaborate funeral car with Lincoln's casket inside

Sixteen gray horses adorned with ostrich plumes

A NATION MOURNS
Tens of thousands of mourners lined the route of Abraham Lincoln's funeral cortege to pay their last respects to the slain president. Lincoln was fifty-six years old at the time of his assassination.

Widow of a martyred president

After so many losses during the Civil War, the newly reunited nation lost its leader just five days after the official end of the conflict. Abraham Lincoln's assassination left the country in shock, and Mary was so grief-stricken that she was unable to leave the White House to attend her husband's funeral.

Mary Lincoln in mourning clothes

Scene depicting Booth shooting Lincoln

A SYMBOL OF SORROW
In Mrs. Lincoln's time, the ritual of mourning someone who died was quite elaborate, and often lasted for years. After the death of a loved one, women wore special clothes and jewelry as a sign of their loss. Among the items worn by the first lady after her husband's death was this somber-looking lapel watch.

IN MEMORIUM
After the president's assassination, objects such as this fan were created to commemorate the terrible tragedy.

Eliza Johnson

AN INVALID WHEN HER HUSBAND TOOK OFFICE, Eliza Johnson rarely left her room in the White House. Still, she contributed a great deal to her husband's career, beginning with teaching Andrew to read and write during the early years of their marriage. Later, as he became active in politics, Eliza raised their five children. During the Civil War, Andrew's Union leanings forced the Johnsons to leave their home in Greeneville, Tennessee, and resettle in Nashville. Eliza, already ill, remained behind after her husband was elected vice president. When he became president after Lincoln's assassination, she did join him in Washington. However, she was a reluctant first lady, and their daughter Martha Johnson Patterson acted as hostess for her father.

A HARD LIFE
The daughter of a poor shoemaker, Eliza McCardle attended school until her teens, but was then obliged to work.

Ticket to Johnson's impeachment trial

AN IMPEACHED PRESIDENT
Andrew Johnson was able to rise from poverty to politics with the help of his wife. After President Lincoln's death, he suddenly found himself in control of the Union. In 1868, Congress tried to impeach Johnson, or remove him from office, because he opposed harsh Congressional policies toward the defeated south. Eliza stood by him throughout this ordeal.

U.S. SENATE
Impeachment of the President
ADMIT THE BEARER
GALLERY.
APRIL 17TH 1868,
Geo. T. Brown
Sergeant-at-Arms.

Martha was the wife of a senator from Tennessee.

A WHITE HOUSE SUBSTITUTE
Martha Johnson Patterson filled in as hostess for her invalid mother, Eliza. Mrs. Patterson was an unassuming woman who remained gracious toward visitors even during her father's impeachment trial.

Julia Grant

BORN IN RURAL MISSOURI, Julia Dent preferred fishing and horseback riding to books. Such spirit appealed to Lieutenant Ulysses S. Grant—he fell in love with her at first sight. After a four-year engagement, during which Ulys, as she called him, distinguished himself as a hero in the Mexican War, the two married in 1848, and had four children. The life of a military wife was difficult, and Julia endured long separations from her husband. During the Civil War, Grant became the leader of the Union army, and his defeat of the Confederate forces enabled the couple to enter the White House on a wave of popularity. With the Union restored, Americans did not criticize the first lady for her lavish dinner parties or expensive purchases as they had Mary Lincoln (p. 22), prompting Mrs. Grant to look back on her four years in the White House as "quite the happiest period of my life."

A WAR HERO CANDIDATE
Ulysses Grant trod a rocky road to success. After resigning from the military in 1854, he tried his hand at various businesses, but failed at each. The Civil War provided him with the perfect chance to return to uniform and prove himself. His success as a presidential candidate was largely due to his fame as a Union general.

Banner from 1868 campaign

JUBILANT JULIA
The first lady was openly delighted to be associated with the capital's rich and famous figures. Sophisticated Washingtonians found her direct manner unpretentious and refreshing.

A LIVELY FAMILY
Well-known Civil War–era photographer Mathew Brady took this portrait of Nelly and Jesse, the Grants' two youngest children. Julia and Ulys's warm and lively brood captivated the American public.

Julia

Ulysses

A SURE BET
Julia supposedly ventured into the Big Bonanza Silver Mine in Nevada after learning that her husband bet she would be afraid to go.

★

Julia Dent Grant

PRESIDENT
Ulysses S. Grant

YEARS AS FIRST LADY
1869–1877

BORN
January 26, 1826
St. Louis, Missouri

MARRIED
August 22, 1848
St. Louis, Missouri

CHILDREN
Frederick Dent
Ulysses Simpson
Ellen Wrenshall
Jesse Root

DIED
Age 76
December 14, 1902
Washington, D.C.

Lucy Hayes

LUCY HAYES ACHIEVED A MILESTONE that set her apart from all of her predecessors. She was the first college graduate to hold the position of first lady. She was also a woman of strong religious and moral beliefs. Although the celebration of the U.S. Centennial was in full swing when the Hayeses took up residence in the White House in 1877, the official festivities were somewhat subdued. A strong supporter of a nineteenth-century movement against alcohol and drugs known as Temperance, Mrs. Hayes, with the full support of her husband, refused to serve liquor in the mansion. Her ban won her the scorn of many and the adoration of the Woman's Christian Temperance Union. It also earned her the memorable nickname Lemonade Lucy. A devoted mother and wife, Mrs. Hayes refused to act as spokesperson for women's rights groups, who had hoped the educated first lady would become their ally.

LEMONADE LUCY
The Woman's Christian Temperance Union commissioned this portrait to honor Lucy Hayes. Although she did not belong to the organization, the first lady's refusal to serve liquor at the White House made her a symbol for women reformers.

Lucy favored simple, dignified dresses rather than high fashion.

A FINE MATCH
Before Lucy Webb ever laid eyes on Rutherford Hayes, she had heard a lot about him. Their mothers, both widows and church friends, conspired to bring the two together. It was a good match. Rutherford, a well-liked and honest president, was also a devoted husband and father.

Lucy Webb's diploma from Wesleyan Female College

THE "NEW WOMAN"
In June 1850, Lucy graduated from Wesleyan Female College in Cincinnati, Ohio. She was not quite twenty years old. In the mid-nineteenth century, a college-educated girl was considered a "new woman." Still, Lucy found that she had only two career options: becoming a wife and a mother. She happily accepted both jobs.

ALL-AMERICAN CHINA
Mrs. Hayes, a popular and diplomatic hostess, helped promote national unity after the Civil War by choosing distinctly American themes, such as this native turkey, for her official White House china. Her unique service also features flowers and scenes from across the country.

Menu and seating plan from a Hayes dinner party

Lucy Webb Hayes

PRESIDENT
Rutherford B. Hayes

YEARS AS FIRST LADY
1877–1881

BORN
August 28, 1831
Chillicothe, Ohio

MARRIED
December 30, 1852
Cincinnati, Ohio

CHILDREN
Birchard Austin
Webb Cook
Rutherford Platt
Joseph Thompson
George Crook
Fanny
Scott Russell
Manning Force

DIED
Age 57
June 25, 1889
Freemont, Ohio

CELEBRATING THE NATION'S BIRTHDAY
Major exhibitions, such as the one advertised in this banner, were held to celebrate the country's one hundredth year of independence from Great Britain. While the first couple maintained a strict routine of morning prayers and evening hymn singing, they encouraged Americans to participate in the various festivities.

The china was designed by Theodore Davis.

MODERN CONVENIENCES
President and Mrs. Hayes found life in the White House easier with the arrival of modern conveniences such as this typewriter. A telephone and a permanent running-water system also made their first appearances in the Executive Mansion during the Hayes administration.

Hatchet

THE OTHER SIDE OF TEMPERANCE
Unlike the first lady, Carry Nation was a controversial Temperance supporter who became famous for entering saloons and smashing barrels of liquor with a hatchet. Seen here with her object of destruction, she went on to found a chapter of the Woman's Christian Temperance Union in Kansas in 1892. One of her Temperance newspapers was named *The Smasher's Mail.*

Bible

Lucretia Garfield

CALLED CRETE BY HER PARENTS, Lucretia Rudolph grew up on a farm in northeast Ohio and met her future husband, James, at school. They endured long separations from each other during the early years of their marriage—first when James left their home in Hiram, Ohio, to serve as state senator in Columbus, and later when he became a lieutenant colonel in the Civil War. Lucretia proudly followed her husband to the White House in 1881. Within months of his term, however, she contracted malaria. Sent to the shore to recuperate, the first lady was shocked to receive a telegram informing her that James had been shot.

CREATIVE CRETE
The first lady's diaries show her to be a wise, independent, and creative woman who acted as an adviser to James. Sadly, she became the first wife of a president to preside at her husband's funeral. She preserved all his political papers for history.

Banner from 1880 campaign

FROM POVERTY TO POLITICS
James Garfield, portrayed on this presidential campaign banner, rose from poverty to become a lawyer, Civil War hero, preacher, and successful politician. His wife kept him from falling prey to scandal and corruption, which had ruined many aspiring politicians of that time. His term in office was cut short by an assassin's bullet.

Satin train

LUCRETIA IN LACE
The first lady wore this gown to the 1881 inaugural ball at what is now the Smithsonian's Arts and Industries Building. The *Washington Post* of March 5, 1881, noted that "Mrs. Garfield's toilet [costume] was a reception dress of delicately shaded lavender satin. The train was finished with a small box plaiting of the same material."

Lace trim

Charles Guiteau

President Garfield

A FATAL SHOT
On July 2, 1881, Charles Guiteau, angered that he could not obtain a federal job, shot the president. A bullet lodged in Garfield's back and the wound became infected. Crete nursed James for more than two months, but medical practices of the time were not advanced enough to save his life.

Ellen Arthur

JUST AS CHESTER ARTHUR'S political career was taking off, his wife, Ellen, died suddenly of pneumonia. Ellen Herndon grew up in and near Washington, D.C., where her father was an officer in the U.S. Navy. Later she had moved to New York City with her widowed mother in 1858. There she met Chester Arthur, a young lawyer who became a Union general during the Civil War. After Arthur became president in 1881, his sister Mary Arthur McElroy served as his official hostess.

Ellen Herndon Arthur

PRESIDENT
Chester A. Arthur

YEARS AS FIRST LADY
Never served as first lady

BORN
August 30, 1837
Fredericksburg, Virginia

MARRIED
October 25, 1859
New York, New York

CHILDREN
William Lewis Herndon
Chester Alan
Ellen

DIED
Age 42
January 12, 1880
New York, New York

ELLEN, KNOWN AS NELL
Ellen Arthur was a fashionable young woman and an accomplished singer. She died suddenly in January 1880—eight months before her husband became president. Chester had a stained glass window installed in her memory at St. John's Episcopal Church, located just opposite the White House.

Arthur was an elegant dresser.

MENDING HIS WAYS
Chester Arthur was known to be a dishonest politician. He might never have been elected president, but Garfield's assassination suddenly landed him a job at the White House. Once in office, he reformed his ways and established the Civil Service Commission, which awarded jobs to workers based on their abilities, not their connections.

UNCONTROLLED GROWTH
During Chester Arthur's administration, the country's population expanded enormously, with new immigrants arriving daily. Leaving poor and unstable conditions in their native lands, passengers on crowded ships such as this one faced uncertain destinies in their new home. The rapid influx of foreigners to American cities strained services to the breaking point and raised tensions among ethnic groups.

Mary Arthur McElroy was Chester Arthur's youngest sister.

ARTHUR'S OFFICIAL HOSTESS
Mary Arthur McElroy served as official hostess during much of her brother's presidency. Chester, however, pined for Nell and never allowed anyone to truly take her place. He often organized official social events himself, and had the White House refurbished by the firm of Tiffany & Co. to suit his elegant tastes.

Frances Cleveland

Ivory satin material

India muslin

HE CALLED HER FRANK and she called him Uncle Cleve. She was a twenty-one-year-old beauty, and he was a forty-eight-year-old bachelor. They were married in the White House—the first wedding of a president to take place in the mansion—and the bride became an overnight sensation. When Frances Folsom wed Grover Cleveland, the former law partner of her deceased father as well as her legal guardian, the press pursued the couple relentlessly. Soon Frances's picture appeared in newspapers, magazines, and advertisements. As first lady, she became a popular object of devotion—an icon. Some historians think that her enormous popularity helped Cleveland, the only president to serve two nonconsecutive terms, return to the White House. And the notoriety did not stop there. The Clevelands' first baby, Ruth, had her own fans, and a candy bar was named in her honor.

THE PICTURE OF BEAUTY
The stunning Frances Folsom became a celebrity when she married portly Grover Cleveland on June 2, 1886. However, because Frances thought it was improper for women to speak out in public, she was never interviewed about her marriage.

EXQUISITE SIMPLICITY
The day after Frances's wedding, the *Washington Post* provided this vivid description of her wedding gown. "The bride wore an enchanting white dress of ivory satin, simply garnished on the high corsage with India muslin crossed in Grecian folds and carried in exquisite falls of simplicity over the petticoat."

A NATIONAL EVENT
The Clevelands tried to keep their wedding private, but it received national media coverage. Engravings such as this were reproduced in popular magazines. However, because journalists were not welcomed at the White House ceremony, the pictures that appeared in the press were based on descriptions provided by guests in attendance.

Dedicated to "President Cleveland and his Accomplished Wife"

Cleveland's Wedding March
HENRY WERNER

MEMORIALIZED IN MUSIC
The Cleveland wedding inspired many songs, including this wedding march.

DEFEAT AND VICTORY

Cleveland was the only president to serve two nonconsecutive terms. After winning the election of 1884—the election from which this campaign banner comes—he lost in 1888, then made a comeback in 1892. Frances joyfully returned to the White House, this time with a baby.

Grover's 1884 campaign was haunted by a scandal: that he had fathered an illegitimate child.

To date, Frances Cleveland is the youngest first lady ever.

WINNING VOTES

When Cleveland ran for reelection in 1888, the Democrats recognized his wife's enormous popularity and used her image on campaign plates, buttons, and posters. That the first lady is pictured on this plate without the president suggests she had enough personal appeal to win public support on her own.

Frances Folsom Cleveland

PRESIDENT
Grover Cleveland

YEARS AS FIRST LADY
1886-1889
1893-1897

BORN
July 21, 1864
Buffalo, New York

MARRIED
June 2, 1886
White House, Washington, D.C.

CHILDREN
Ruth
Esther
Marion
Richard Folsom
Francis Grover

DIED
Age 83
October 29, 1947
Baltimore, Maryland

Frances Cleveland

Grover Cleveland

THE QUEEN OF DIAMONDS

The image of Mrs. Cleveland appeared everywhere, even on such unlikely objects as playing cards. While her popularity helped her husband politically, the president became incensed by the threat to his family's privacy. He tried to stop Frances's likeness from being used in advertising. However, a bill he supported concerning the commercial use of celebrities' names and images without their written consent did not pass.

The first lady was seen as a symbol of domestic happiness. Often her image was used to counter the rising women's movement.

Sewing thread

A NATURAL-BORN HOSTESS

As first lady, Frances performed the job of hostess so well that Republicans thought her a threat to their party. Even at his bride's first White House reception, Grover had been so pleased with her social grace that he playfully announced to her mother, "She'll do!" Frances's popularity increased as a result of the Saturday receptions she hosted for working women, who could not visit the White House during the week.

AN ADVERTISING GIMMICK

Produced by the Merrick Thread Company, this ad shows the image of the first couple bound in a heart of thread to suggest that marital love keeps the country united. On a different level, it reveals how shamelessly advertisers used Frances's image to sell products.

Caroline Harrison

CAROLINE SCOTT was just a teenager when she met Benjamin Harrison, whose grandfather had been the ninth president of the United States. While he embarked on a political career, Caroline distinguished herself as a volunteer for the sick and orphaned. Once in the White House, she managed to pursue her own interests while using her influence as first lady to advance worthy causes. She was the first president general of the Daughters of the American Revolution and became a fund-raiser for the Johns Hopkins University Medical School—after they agreed to accept female students. Caroline died in the White House in 1892, leaving her daughter, Mary McKee, to act as hostess during the last months of her father's term.

CREATIVE CARRIE
A White House visitor recalled that Mrs. Harrison, nicknamed Carrie, applied her skills in music, art, and design to create an atmosphere of "genteel gaiety."

Goldenrod pattern, designed by an Indiana artist

Caroline   *Russell*   *Benjamin*   *Mary*

THE HARRISON HOUSEHOLD
The Harrisons had two children. Their son was a frequent visitor to the White House, and their daughter and her family lived there. Caroline was a caring supporter of many public causes, but the president was said to be so cold mannered that people called him the Human Iceberg.

AT THE TOP OF HER CLASS
Mrs. Harrison's father, who spent most of his career as a mathematics professor, believed in providing a good education for his daughters. In 1849, he established the Oxford Female Institute in southern Ohio, from which Carrie, a fine student, received this diploma.

Brocaded fabric, woven in New York

A GOLDENROD GOWN
Mary McKee wore this gown to the 1889 inaugural ball at Washington's Pension Building. A pattern of goldenrod—her father's favorite flower—is woven into the fabric.

A HOUSE FIT FOR A FIRST FAMILY
This photograph of one of the rooms in the White House was taken about the time Carrie modernized the mansion.

★

Caroline Scott Harrison

PRESIDENT
Benjamin Harrison

YEARS AS FIRST LADY
1889–1892

BORN
October 1, 1832
Oxford, Ohio

MARRIED
October 20, 1853
Oxford, Ohio

CHILDREN
Russell Benjamin
Mary Scott

DIED
Age 60
October 25, 1892
Washington, D.C.

Ida McKinley

IDA MCKINLEY WAS BOTH BEAUTIFUL and well educated. She attended private schools and later learned about business from her father, a wealthy banker. These strong qualities won her the attention of William McKinley. However, Ida's life took a tragic turn after her marriage. The deaths of her mother in 1873 and then only months later her infant daughter brought on a nervous breakdown, followed by epileptic seizures. Because of her delicate condition, which was never mentioned publicly, Ida's appearance at official functions was awkward. Unable to walk, she was often carried into rooms to receive visitors, and remained seated, propped up on pillows. Strangely, after her husband was shot in 1901, Ida's seizures disappeared.

Ida Saxton McKinley

PRESIDENT
William McKinley

YEARS AS FIRST LADY
1897–1901

BORN
June 8, 1847
Canton, Ohio

MARRIED
January 25, 1871
Canton, Ohio

CHILDREN
Katherine
Ida

DIED
Age 59
May 26, 1907
Canton, Ohio

A DIFFICULT WIFE
As a young woman, Ida was willful and accustomed to getting her own way. As first lady, she was a demanding invalid, whose husband nonetheless remained devoted to her.

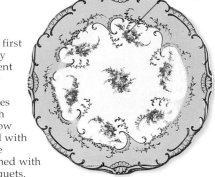

Mother of pearl

Silk fabric

A SENSE OF STYLE
Ida's affliction made social events a burden, but she refused to delegate her duties to an official hostess. The first lady owned a wardrobe of elegant gowns and fashionable accessories, such as this fan, to keep up appearances for White House visitors.

BADGE OF SUPPORT
Voters from Canton, Ohio, who wore this badge during McKinley's 1896 presidential campaign proved that a political wife could develop her own local following. Ida believed William was a great man, and did all she could to advance his career.

PREFERENCE FOR FLOWERS
During her time as first lady, Mrs. McKinley used several different sets of china, many of which had floral designs. These plates are made of English porcelain. The yellow border is decorated with gold, and the white ground is embellished with pink and blue bouquets.

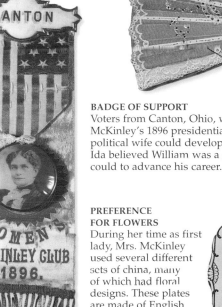

Pink and blue flowers

MEMORIAL MUSIC
On September 6, 1901, President McKinley was killed by an anarchist, a person who opposes any form of government. His assassination prompted the composition of memorial works, such as this song.

Edith Roosevelt

EDITH KERMIT CAROW and Teddy Roosevelt were childhood playmates, but it was not until he was a widower with a young daughter that they married. After her husband's election to the presidency in 1900, Edith presided over a complete restoration of the White House and added the West Wing for presidential offices. She also paid special tribute to the women who had preceded her there by creating a picture gallery of first ladies in the White House. Well aware of the public's fascination with the wild antics of her six rambunctious children, Mrs. Roosevelt became the *first* first lady to hire a social secretary to help control the image of her family.

ROUGH RIDER
When the Spanish-American War broke out in 1898, Theodore promptly assembled a volunteer cavalry regiment known as the Rough Riders. Their victorious charge up Cuba's San Juan Hill led to a Spanish surrender and earned Roosevelt hero status. Edith tolerated, and even enjoyed, her husband's love of adventure.

THE CALM IN THE STORM
Edith remained calm and dignified while her children created havoc in the White House. Whether her young sons were leading their pony through the mansion's corridors or sliding down the staircase, she was in control. By 1901, reporters were regularly briefed on the activities of the first family.

Painted wood

A MOOSE ON WHEELS
TR, as Roosevelt was called, hunted big game, but his grandchildren contented themselves with this pull-toy moose. They played with it at Sagamore Hill, the family's Long Island estate.

Edith Roosevelt's name stamped on the flap

PRINCESS ALICE
The only person Edith could not totally control was Alice, her beautiful and rebellious stepdaughter. Known as Princess Alice, the headstrong girl dared to smoke in public.

A WORLD TRAVELER
The first lady carried this well-worn leather attaché case on a trip to Panama with the president and later on journeys to Europe and Brazil.

★

Edith Kermit Carow Roosevelt

PRESIDENT
Theodore Roosevelt

YEARS AS FIRST LADY
1901–1909

BORN
August 6, 1861
Norwich, Connecticut

MARRIED
December 2, 1886
London, England

CHILDREN
Alice Lee (stepdaughter)
Theodore
Kermit
Ethel Carow
Archibald Bulloch
Quentin

DIED
Age 87
September 30, 1948
Oyster Bay, New York

Helen Taft

As a child, Helen Herron dreamed of being first lady. An independent young woman, she formed her own salon, or intellectual group, at the age of twenty-two and invited a young attorney by the name of William Taft to join. The two married several years later. While Helen raised their family, Will served as a superior court judge in Cincinnati, Ohio, and then as U.S. governor to the Philippines. Just two months into Taft's presidency, Helen suffered a stroke. Still, the first lady managed to put her own stamp on the White House.

Helen Herron Taft

PRESIDENT
William H. Taft

YEARS AS FIRST LADY
1909–1913

BORN
June 2, 1861
Cincinnati, Ohio

MARRIED
June 19, 1886
Cincinnati, Ohio

CHILDREN
Robert Alphonso
Helen
Charles Phelps II

DIED
Age 82
May 22, 1943
Washington, D.C.

AMBITIOUS NELLIE
Helen, called Nellie, showed more enthusiasm for her husband's Philippines post than he did. Aware that the experience would be both exciting and exotic, she also hoped it would lead him to the presidency.

BREAKING WITH TRADITION
Nellie played an important role in Will's rise to the presidency. Perhaps that is why the elated first lady broke with tradition on inauguration day by riding with her husband from the swearing-in ceremony at the U.S. Capitol to the White House. Previous first ladies had followed behind in a separate vehicle.

Fur trim

Fleece lining

Goldfish and lotus designs

William

Helen

CHINESE ROBE
Helen's Manchu-style coat was meant to be worn in cold weather, although the embroidered lotus and goldfish motifs are symbols of spring and summer. The fur trim was added later. While living in the Philippines, Mrs. Taft made a trip to China to escape the tropical heat, and may have purchased the coat there.

SIGNS OF THE TIMES
As a sign that the nation was changing from an agrarian—or farming—culture to an industrialized one, the Tafts' cow was the last one to graze on the White House lawn. The president and first lady also purchased the first White House motorcar.

A LOVELY LEGACY
The thousands of Japanese cherry trees that bloom along the Potomac River each spring are the legacy of Helen Taft, who had them planted in the nation's capital.

Ellen Wilson

GRACIOUS AND INTELLIGENT, Ellen Wilson brought a quiet southern charm to the White House. The Savannah, Georgia, native was an accomplished painter, a lover of literature, and a devoted mother to three daughters. When her husband, Woodrow, embarked on his political career, she smoothed the way by helping him edit and rehearse speeches as well as by advising him on the issues. Like many women at the time of the First World War, Mrs. Wilson believed in improving living conditions in the nation's cities. In fact, she supported a bill in Congress having to do with slum clearance. Called the Ellen Wilson Bill, it passed in 1914, shortly before her death from an incurable kidney ailment.

A PERFECT PARTNER
Ellen Wilson is largely credited for her husband's success. She proved to be the perfect partner for a man who needed the support and encouragement of a devoted wife.

U.S. Capitol

WIN WITH WILSON
Ellen wholeheartedly supported Woodrow's rise in politics. She was delighted with his presidential win in 1912, the election from which this campaign pennant comes. Wilson was a man of strong ideals, whose struggle to prevent American involvement in World War I failed. The United States eventually entered the conflict in 1917.

Wilson campaign pennant

Margaret

Jessie

Eleanor

Ellen

Woodrow

THE WILSONS AT HOME
Before entering political life, Woodrow Wilson was a popular professor at Princeton University in New Jersey. There, Ellen raised the couple's three daughters—Margaret, Jessie, and Eleanor. This photograph was taken in 1911, after Wilson left academia to serve as governor of New Jersey.

THE ELLEN WILSON BILL
Photographer Lewis Hine took this photograph of an alley dwelling in Washington, D.C., in 1908. Shocked by the deplorable state of living conditions in alleys such as this just beyond the U.S. Capitol, the first lady became an advocate for housing reform.

Edith Wilson

THE GATEKEEPER
Edith Wilson screened her ailing husband's visitors and mail. The press often thought her influence on the executive office was excessive, and called it a "regency."

EDITH BOLLING received no formal schooling until her teenage years, but she went on to become one of America's most influential first ladies. Born and raised in rural Virginia, she moved to Washington, D.C., in 1896, shortly after marrying Norman Galt, the manager of a prosperous jewelry store. Edith mingled with the Washington elite, traveled abroad, and bought the finest fashions. Her husband's sudden death in 1908 left her a wealthy widow. Years later, a chance encounter with the recently widowed Woodrow Wilson resulted in her marriage and move to the White House. When the president suffered a paralyzing stroke in 1918, Edith was accused of running the government single-handedly.

MRS. WILSON AT HOME
"At home" cards, such as this one for Mrs. Wilson, announced the days and times when a first lady wished to receive visitors at the White House.

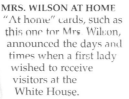

Mrs Wilson
At Home
Friday afternoon
May 23rd
from five until seven o'clock

Initials standing for Young Women's Christian Association

GIFTS OF PEACE
This pin and box were presented to Mrs. Wilson by the people of Paris in 1919, when she traveled with Woodrow to France for the peace negotiations after the end of World War I. Edith was the *first* first lady to accompany a president on an official visit abroad.

Diamonds

Lalique glass doves

Lalique glass box

THE SECOND LINE OF DEFENSE
American women made an important contribution to the war effort, as this YWCA poster from World War I proudly boasts. The first lady played a critical and extraordinary role, too. At the urging of her husband, she decoded secret diplomatic and military messages sent from Europe to the president.

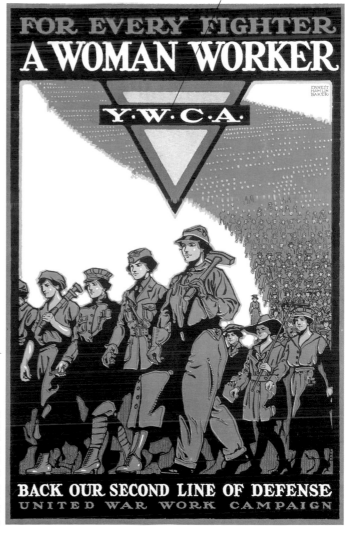

FOR EVERY FIGHTER
A WOMAN WORKER
Y·W·C·A·
BACK OUR SECOND LINE OF DEFENSE
UNITED WAR WORK CAMPAIGN

Mrs. Wilson and the Nineteenth Amendment

Although the United States is a democracy, women were not legally permitted to vote until 1920. Feeling deprived of this basic right of citizenship, women began to fight for it in the mid-1800s. The nineteenth-century suffrage—or right-to-vote—movement was led by feminists such as Lucretia Mott, Elizabeth Cady Stanton, and Susan B. Anthony. In the early twentieth century, they picketed, lobbied, marched, and petitioned Congress until their voices were heard. Despite the fact that she was one of the nation's most powerful first ladies, Edith Wilson opposed the suffrage movement. Even so, the Nineteenth Amendment, by which women won the right to vote, was passed during Wilson's administration.

Suffrage sash over armor

MARCHING ON TO VICTORY
Support for the suffrage movement took many forms. This sheet music was dedicated to the suffragists of the world. The cover depicts a suffrage herald who raises her trumpet to announce a new day.

A CRUSADER'S CAPE
An early twentieth-century suffragist wore this cape and sash. Women suffragists adopted this uniform to show their solidarity and gain publicity for their cause.

The procession drew five to eight thousand marchers.

U.S. Capitol

Purple, white, and gold were the colors of the militant wing of the suffrage crusade.

Suffrage herald

A MARCH ON WASHINGTON
Suffrage supporters held a parade in Washington, D.C., on March 3, 1913, just one day before the Wilsons moved into the White House. Angry spectators attacked many marchers—roughing them up and spitting on them—and the U.S. Cavalry was needed to restore order. This is the official program from that procession.

Button of the National Woman Suffrage Association

VOTES FOR WOMEN

White House gate

Button of a pro-suffrage women's club

HOUSEWIVES LEAGUE

THE PRO FACTION

Women needed men to support suffrage as well; without their votes, the Nineteenth Amendment would never pass in Congress. As such, they launched a nationwide political campaign to win public approval, producing buttons, banners, and other propaganda—materials that helped further their cause.

MR. PRESIDENT HOW LONG MUST WOMEN WAIT FOR LIBERTY

YANK the PLANK

YANK THE PLANK

The suffragists had a political platform—a declaration of their beliefs—for which they hoped to win support. Those opposed to their platform, or plank, wanted it dropped, or yanked, from the Congress. This banner boldly states their desire.

WOMEN HAVE NO RIGHT TO VOTE

Anti-suffrage buttons

THE ANTIS

Many people joined Edith Wilson in opposition to suffrage. These "antis," or anti-suffragists, felt that giving wives and mothers political influence would threaten domestic harmony. However, the amendment was finally added to the U.S. Constitution on August 26, 1920.

ANTI SUFFRAGE

HOW LONG MUST WOMEN WAIT

In January 1917, a group of radical suffragists known as the National Woman's Party began picketing in front of the White House. This infuriated Mrs. Wilson, who nevertheless sent word for them to come in from the cold. They refused her invitation. The group was later arrested for disturbing the peace. Hundreds of suffragists were sent to jail for picketing the White House.

Florence Harding

THE DAUGHTER of a successful businessman, Florence Kling was strong-willed and self-reliant. In 1880, at age nineteen, she eloped with the son of a coal dealer, who soon showed himself to be an alcoholic. When her husband abandoned her and their newborn son, she supported herself by giving piano lessons. Years later, she met Warren Harding, then editor of the local newspaper in Marion, Ohio. She and Warren were married just a month before her thirty-first birthday. While Warren used his newspaper to make political connections, his wife ran the circulation department. Later, she took credit for managing his presidential campaign. Unfortunately, a scandal regarding government corruption shrouded her reign in the White House, which was cut short by Warren's death in 1923.

HARD TIMES FOR HARDING
The unassuming but likable Warren Harding used poor judgment in choosing advisers, and as a result, his administration was weakened by charges of scandal and corruption.

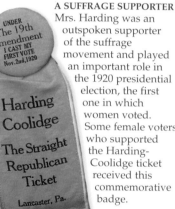

A SUFFRAGE SUPPORTER
Mrs. Harding was an outspoken supporter of the suffrage movement and played an important role in the 1920 presidential election, the first one in which women voted. Some female voters who supported the Harding-Coolidge ticket received this commemorative badge.

THE DUCHESS
A misunderstood woman who was both admired and ridiculed for her folksy midwestern style, Mrs. Harding was called the Duchess by her husband and his friends.

FLAPPER STYLE
Florence Harding's flapper-style dress, created by New York designer Harry Collins, was the height of fashion during the 1920s. The first lady wore it to the 1921 inauguration ceremony.

THE FIRST LADY OF THE LAND
Dated March 4, 1921, this sheet music honors the new first lady. Mrs. Harding served as her husband's unofficial campaign manager and once said, "I know what's best for the president. I put him in the White House."

Pearlized sequins over delicate tulle

★

Florence Kling Harding

PRESIDENT
Warren G. Harding

YEARS AS FIRST LADY
1921–1923

BORN
August 15, 1860
Marion, Ohio

MARRIED
July 8, 1891
Marion, Ohio

CHILDREN FROM FORMER MARRIAGE
Marshall deWolfe

DIED
Age 64
November 21, 1924
Marion, Ohio

Grace Coolidge

UNLIKE HER HUSBAND, who was nicknamed Silent Cal, Grace Coolidge was sweet and sociable. She grew up in Burlington, Vermont, attended the University of Vermont, and then moved to Northampton, Massachusetts, to teach at the Clarke School for the Deaf. It was there that she met and married Calvin, then a lawyer. As his political career took off, Grace stayed at home with their two sons, even playing baseball with them in their father's absence. Warren Harding's death in 1923 catapulted Coolidge to the presidency and Grace into the public eye. Her years as first lady were marred by the death of her younger son, Calvin, Jr. Yet Grace managed to shine in the White House.

AN ANIMAL LOVER
During her years as first lady, Mrs. Coolidge populated the White House with many unusual pets, including this raccoon named Rebecca.

AN OCCASIONAL EXTRAVAGANCE
Although Calvin Coolidge was old-fashioned and frugal, his one extravagance was to buy his wife beautiful and stylish clothing to set off her good looks.

Turquoise

Silver

JEWELRY WITH A SPECIAL MEANING
The first lady wore this silver-and-turquoise bracelet of Native American design. Calvin had Indian ancestors and considered his membership in the Sioux tribe a great honor.

SILENT CAL
Calvin Coolidge was an honest man who rarely smiled and seldom spoke. Grace liked to tell this story about her unusually quiet husband: A Washington hostess once bet Coolidge that she could make him say more than two words. The president replied, "You lose."

Grace Coolidge dress from the 1920s

AN ADVOCATE FOR THE DEAF
Grace welcomed Helen Keller, who was both deaf and blind, to the White House on January 11, 1926. In order to "hear" the first lady when she spoke, Keller placed one hand on Mrs. Coolidge's neck and held the other one to her lips.

Lou Hoover

E QUESTRIENNE, HUNTER, TAXIDERMIST, and linguist—Lou was a woman of many interests. She was also the first woman to graduate with a degree in geology from Stanford University. Shortly after completing her studies, she married Herbert Hoover, a mining engineer she had met at college. His business took them to posts around the world. During World War I and throughout the Great Depression, which began in 1929, Lou devoted herself to public service. While in the White House, she lent financial and moral support to the causes of women's and civil rights, but without stepping outside of the traditional role of first lady.

THE LIGHTER SIDE OF LOU
Generally a quiet companion to her husband when in public, Mrs. Hoover once showed her sense of humor by commenting, "I enjoy campaigning because my husband makes the speeches—and I receive the roses."

The driver is made of painted cast iron.

A WHITE HOUSE CHRISTMAS
On December 24, 1929, a fire broke out in the Executive Mansion. The following Christmas, the first lady gave White House visitors toy fire engines as remembrances of that event. The truck is made of heavy cast metal and has wheels that actually turn.

The wheels were cast separately and spin on axles.

A SELF-MADE MAN
Herbert Hoover was an American success story. He grew up an orphan and became a millionaire. During World War I, Herbert served as an effective administrator of humanitarian aid to Europe.

Herbert's promise to speed up recovery did not work with voters.

SPEED UP RECOVERY
RE-ELECT
HOOVER
KEEP HIM
ON THE JOB

THE GREAT DEPRESSION
On October 24, 1929, the New York Stock Market crashed, triggering the Great Depression. Many people lost their jobs, as well as their life savings. President Hoover was blamed—unfairly, Lou thought—for the plight of the country. Although he tried to boost the nation's hopes for recovery, Herbert lost his bid for reelection in 1932.

Button from 1932 campaign

The Girl Scout's Promise

On my honor
I will try

To do my Duty to
God and my Country

To help other People
at all times

To Obey the
Scout Laws

Season's Greetings

Christmas card from the Hoovers

Scout's honor

An advocate for active and self-reliant women, Lou Hoover was a great supporter of the Girl Scouts and promoted the organization by inviting troop members to the White House. She had a long-term commitment to the group, having been sworn in as a troop leader by the founder, Juliette Lowe, in 1917. In 1922, Lou was elected national president and as first lady became the Girl Scouts' honorary national president. Mrs. Hoover's involvement with the group enabled her to offer progressive views about women's self-esteem and leadership abilities without appearing too political.

126,515,000 Girl Scouts stamps were issued.

STAMP OF APPROVAL
The U.S. Postal Service issued this stamp on July 24, 1962, to honor and promote the Girl Scouts of America.

4c U.S. POSTAGE GIRL SCOUTS · U.S.A.

PRESIDENT'S WIFE STRESSES VITAL PART SCOUTING PLAYS IN LIFE OF TODAY'S GIRLHOOD

SPEAKING UP FOR GIRLS
During her term as first lady, Mrs. Hoover was a distinguished guest at the National Girl Scouts Convention. She frequently spoke to girls of the value of social service and volunteerism, two lifelong commitments of her own. This headline is from the *Virginia Pilot and Norfolk Landmark*, dated October 8, 1932.

ON THE AIR
On March 24, 1931, the first lady addressed the nation's Girl Scouts by radio, thanking them on behalf of herself and the president for their outstanding efforts to help the needy. Lou was the first presidential wife to use radio to promote her views.

★

Lou Henry Hoover

PRESIDENT
Herbert Hoover

YEARS AS FIRST LADY
1929–1933

BORN
March 29, 1874
Waterloo, Iowa

MARRIED
February 10, 1899
Monterey, California

CHILDREN
Herbert Clark
Allan Henry

DIED
Age 69
January 7, 1944
New York, New York

Eleanor Roosevelt

THE CHILD OF EXTRAORDINARILY attractive and wealthy parents, the young Eleanor Roosevelt was tormented by her lack of beauty. Her mother died when she was eight and her father, whom she adored, died two years later. Raised by her grandmother and educated at the best private schools, Eleanor married her charming fifth cousin Franklin Delano Roosevelt. After bearing six children, one of whom died in infancy, she devoted her life to politics, advancing Franklin's career after he contracted polio. During the Great Depression, Mrs. Roosevelt's trips across the United States, as well as her weekly radio broadcasts, brought hope to millions of suffering Americans.

A "USEFUL" FIRST LADY
Eleanor went from being "a solemn child . . . entirely lacking in the spontaneous joy and mirth of youth" to being an ambitious first lady who early on in her husband's first term confided, "There may be ways in which I can be useful."

Eleanor, already a Roosevelt, did not have to change her name after marriage.

Franklin

Eleanor

James

Anna

THE ROOSEVELT FAMILY
The young and privileged Roosevelts—who were distant cousins as well as husband and wife—are seen here with their two oldest children, Anna and James.

FDR
Franklin Delano Roosevelt, called FDR, was the only president to serve three terms in office. Despite being crippled by polio in 1921, at age thirty-nine, he was able to perform the tasks of the presidency, due in large part to the efforts of his extraordinary wife.

A POPULAR POLITICAL WIFE
An effective campaigner, Eleanor accompanied her husband on the campaign trail, pausing whenever possible to shake hands with supporters from the train. Although she was raised to think campaigning was inappropriate for women, she did so to help Franklin, whose illness made him tire easily.

A NATION'S HUNGER
The first lady felt anguish for those who went hungry during the Great Depression. In this photograph from 1932, she serves food to the needy at a soup kitchen in New York City.

Eleanor's initials appear on the clasp.

This belt is a reproduction.

CLOTHES BEFITTING A FIRST LADY
Eleanor wore this velvet day dress to her husband's first inauguration on March 4, 1933. This shade of lavender is called Eleanor blue. After her White House years, Mrs. Roosevelt donned this mink coat on special occasions. It has a gold clasp inscribed with her initials.

THE NEW DEAL
The New Deal, which is promoted in this patriotic sheet music, was a federal program designed to get people back to work after the Great Depression.

President Franklin Roosevelt

A wartime ambassador

Eleanor used her great skill as a communicator to calm the fears of the American public and boost morale during World War II. Following America's entry into the conflict in December 1941, she traveled a record number of miles around the world to visit U.S. troops, bringing notes home from soldiers and then passing them on to their worried families. In October 1942, she became the only first lady to fly by herself across the Atlantic. While in Europe, she toured the heavily bombed sections of London, visited women's training centers, and inspected American Red Cross units. By serving as unofficial ambassador for the president, she made a great contribution to the nation's war effort.

A BEARER OF GOODWILL
Mrs. R., as Eleanor was often called, extended her influence beyond the home front during World War II. Her presence abroad gave U.S. forces hope and kept up their spirits. Here, she visits troops stationed in Central America.

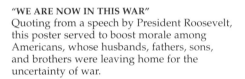

This poster quotes FDR.

"WE ARE NOW IN THIS WAR"
Quoting from a speech by President Roosevelt, this poster served to boost morale among Americans, whose husbands, fathers, sons, and brothers were leaving home for the uncertainty of war.

The first lady as social activist

Called the First Lady of the World by President Harry S. Truman, Eleanor Roosevelt was one of the greatest humanitarians of the twentieth century. As first lady, she worked tirelessly to improve the lives of the underprivileged. After being widowed at age sixty, she continued to serve her country as the U.S. delegate to the United Nations. Eleanor was also a firm advocate of civil rights, and fought to end segregation and discrimination. Remembered for her great compassion, Mrs. Roosevelt remains one of the most respected first ladies.

Eleanor on her wedding day

Eleanor as a young woman

Eleanor as a child

Eleanor in later life

HONORING A SPECIAL WOMAN
This quilt, sewn by Callie Fanning Smith in 1940, was made to honor the first lady. It is composed of cloth squares featuring portraits of Eleanor Roosevelt and scenes from her life.

Conductor
and pianist
Leonard Bernstein

A WAY WITH WORDS
Mrs. Roosevelt was an accomplished writer and used this desk when working at her Val-Kill cottage in New York. During the Depression, she wrote a column called "My Day," which appeared in hundreds of newspapers. She also wrote a best-selling book about her early life.

SPEAKING UP FOR CIVIL RIGHTS
In 1939, Marian Anderson, a world-famous singer, was prohibited from performing at the Daughters of the American Revolution's Constitution Hall because she was African American. The first lady withdrew her membership in the organization in protest. She then helped arrange a concert for Marian on the steps of the Lincoln Memorial.

*133,170,000 stamps
were issued.*

A DECLARATION OF HUMAN RIGHTS
Eleanor did not stop her humanitarian and political work after her husband's death. Harry Truman, Franklin's successor as president, gave her a post with the United Nations. She was the primary architect of the U.N.'s Universal Declaration of Human Rights, which set forth the basic principles of human rights in the modern world. Mrs. Roosevelt worked at the U.N. until she was almost seventy years old. Even in her later years, she continued to travel and advance these concerns.

A MODEL AMERICAN
Mrs. Roosevelt's work continues to influence and inspire Americans. Among the many honors bestowed on her is this five-cent stamp, issued in her memory in 1963.

*The declaration was
adopted in 1948.*

Bess Truman

AFTER HARRY TRUMAN left the White House, he declared that his wife had been his "chief adviser" and a "full partner." Indeed, Bess had worked alongside her husband even before he entered politics; and when he became a U.S. senator in 1935, she willingly left her hometown of Independence, Missouri, to take up life in the nation's capital. There, she became a paid staff member in Harry's office. When Franklin Roosevelt died in office in 1945, Vice President Harry Truman took up the challenge of running the country—and his wife faced the predicament of unwanted fame.

A PRIVATE FIRST LADY
Mrs. Truman, who disliked social functions and held no press conferences, was respected as a no-nonsense woman and loyal wife.

★

Elizabeth Wallace Truman

PRESIDENT
Harry S. Truman

YEARS AS FIRST LADY
1945–1953

BORN
February 13, 1885
Independence, Missouri

MARRIED
June 28, 1919
Independence, Missouri

CHILDREN
Margaret

DIED
Age 97
October 18, 1982
Independence, Missouri

Badge from 1948 campaign

"THE BUCK STOPS HERE"
Harry Truman coined this phrase and also included it in a sign he kept on his desk. This symbolized his devotion to the office and the seriousness with which he carried out his presidential responsibilities. One of his most difficult duties was to bring about the end of World War II with the decision to drop atomic bombs on two Japanese cities.

THE BOSS'S DRESS
Mrs. Truman, whose husband called her the Boss, wore this dress to the inaugural reception on January 20, 1949. It was designed by Polo Gowns of Paris and New York.

Pearl gray damask with gold thread

Presidential seal

WHISTLE-STOP CAMPAIGNING
Harry Truman charmed the crowds during his 1948 reelection campaign, but Bess generally shied away from media attention. This is a rare photograph of her campaigning with her husband from the back platform of a train.

PRESIDENTIAL CHINA
In 1951, the Trumans purchased a set of china for use in the White House. The plates have a green border edged in gold.

Mamie Eisenhower

As the wife of a career military officer who lived in the jungles of Panama as well as in small towns across the United States, Mamie Eisenhower had years of experience in handling challenging social situations. This served her well when Dwight D. Eisenhower, the former supreme allied commander of U.S. forces in Europe during World War II, became president. Mamie's early childhood, however, had been comfortable and carefree. The charming girl was spoiled by her father, John Doud, who had earned enough money in the meatpacking business to retire in his thirties. Although her father expressed concern that his indulged daughter would not be happy as a soldier's wife, Mamie was intent on marrying Dwight, and lived up to the task.

A DISTINCTIVE FIRST LADY
Mamie, whose bangs created a stir, put her personal stamp on the White House as well. The first lady furnished her private quarters with pink pillows and bath towels, and tried to make the Executive Mansion a cozy home for her husband and herself.

A CHARMED LIFE
Each of the thirty-four charms on Mamie's bracelet represent meaningful events that occurred in Ike's life.

West Point insignia

Four-leaf clover for luck

Jeep with "Ike" on hood

PI for Philippine Island service

LIKABLE IKE
Dwight, nicknamed Ike, was an optimistic man who was openly affectionate toward his wife. Americans were fond of him, too, and enjoyed the prosperity that accompanied his presidency.

They liked Ike's wife!
Mamie, a devoted wife, mother, and hostess, appealed to Americans, and particularly to housewives who felt they had something in common with the most visible woman in the country. On the campaign trail, she became a celebrity in her own right. As first lady, Mamie tackled her role with enthusiasm, ran the White House with military precision, and charmed the nation at the same time.

MAMIE Prosperity

A POLITICAL PIG
The Santa Barbara (California) Republican Women's Organization sold this piggy bank as a fund-raising item in 1956. It came with instructions to "Take Me Home and Feed Me Well!"

MAMIE PAT

POPULAR WITH THE PUBLIC
As this campaign button shows, Mamie Eisenhower and Pat Nixon—the wives of the presidential and vice presidential candidates of 1952 and 1956—had a lot of appeal with voters. They were especially popular with women, who by the 1950s were voting in equal numbers with men.

Mamie's personalized cooler

1952 Republican National Convention Chicago Illinois
MRS. IKE EISENHOWER

Jacqueline Kennedy

THE GLAMOROUS AND PRIVILEGED Jacqueline Kennedy—Jackie to the American public—became a symbol of style and elegance during the 1960s. Young, wealthy, intelligent, and beautiful, she may have been her husband's greatest asset during his campaign for president in 1960. Raised on an estate in the resort town of Southampton, Long Island, and in a Park Avenue townhouse in New York City, she had her own pony just months after she could walk. Twin interests in writing and art steered her to a career in journalism after college. While working as a photographer for the *Washington Times-Herald*, Jackie met a witty and handsome young congressman from Massachusetts named John F. Kennedy. Their storybook wedding in 1953 drew thousands of reporters and onlookers.

Jack Bouvier

Jackie Bouvier

John Bouvier

THE JACKIE LOOK
As a young woman, Jackie was noted for her beauty and style. Later, as first lady, her fashion sense influenced public taste and inspired a new look.

A CHILDHOOD PASSION
Wearing riding jodhpurs, Jackie accompanied her father and grandfather to the Maidstone Club in East Hampton in the late 1930s. Jackie's father, Jack Bouvier, was a wealthy Wall Street stockbroker, and her mother was an accomplished equestrienne. Following her mother's lead, Jackie won two national horsemanship competitions by age seven. Her other childhood passion came from her grandfather, John Bouvier, who inspired her to read and write poetry.

ON ASSIGNMENT
With this bulky camera in hand, Jackie pursued interesting stories throughout the nation's capital. She interviewed truck drivers and congressmen, laborers and actresses. Her column was accompanied by black-and-white photographs, which she developed herself.

Jackie's Graflex camera

THE INQUIRING CAMERA GIRL
After winning first prize in a *Vogue* magazine writing contest, twenty-one-year-old Jacqueline Bouvier considered a career in journalism. In late 1951, she was offered a position with the *Washington Times-Herald* newspaper and in early 1952 became the paper's "Inquiring Camera Girl," earning $42.50 per week.

★

Jacqueline Bouvier Kennedy

PRESIDENT
John F. Kennedy

YEARS AS FIRST LADY
1961–1963

BORN
July 28, 1929
Southampton, New York

MARRIED
September 12, 1953
Newport, Rhode Island

CHILDREN
Caroline Bouvier
John Fitzgerald
Patrick Bouvier

DIED
Age 64
May 19, 1994
New York, New York

Ivory silk wedding gown with portrait neckline

2.88-carat diamond

2.84-carat emerald

AN EXTRAORDINARY ENGAGEMENT
While working at the newspaper, Jackie met the man she later referred to as "the choicest bachelor in the Senate." John F. Kennedy, called Jack, was the son of a millionaire, a Harvard University graduate, and a World War II hero. They were engaged in the summer of 1953.

THE FAIRY TALE BEGINS
On September 12, 1953, twenty-four-year-old Jacqueline Bouvier married the thirty-six-year-old senator from Massachusetts, John Kennedy. Thousands of reporters and spectators jostled for position outside St. Mary's Roman Catholic Church in Newport, Rhode Island, for a glimpse of the newlyweds. After the ceremony, there was an outdoor reception at Hammersmith Farm, the estate of Jackie's stepfather, Hugh Auchincloss. More than twelve hundred guests—members of high society as well as politicians—attended.

Continued from previous page

A youthful White House

Although in private the Kennedy marriage was not always happy, Jack and Jackie radiated contentment and optimism to the public, and skillfully used the media to help promote that image. The Kennedys were often photographed with their two children and appeared the model American family. Upon entering the White House, Jackie soon proved that she was ambitious and effective beyond the domestic sphere. She used her knowledge of art and her position as first lady to initiate a restoration project that transformed the White House into a national showcase, and welcomed noted writers, scientists, and politicians to participate in state receptions.

Jackie

John, Jr.

Caroline

Jack

Badge from Kennedy's inauguration

A NEW VOICE
John Kennedy wooed voters with confidence and charm. His memorable inaugural address urged Americans, "Ask not what your country can do for you—ask what you can do for your country."

THE FIRST FAMILY
Mrs. Kennedy was delighted with the birth of Caroline in 1957 and John, Jr., in 1960. She once told an interviewer, "If you bungle raising your children nothing else much matters in life." She was determined to shelter her son and daughter from the attention directed at them by their father's position. However, commercial products, such as this comic book, did appear with their likenesses.

Caroline Kennedy

AMERICA'S FIRST YOUNG LADY!
CAROLINE KENNEDY
A Charlton Publication

Gray brocade jacket

A-line dress

SETTING A TREND
Jackie wore this suit designed by Oleg Cassini to a White House function in 1961. Women were so captivated with her fashion style that department stores used mannequins bearing her features and hairstyle.

After Camelot

President Kennedy was assassinated in Dallas, Texas, on November 22, 1963. The press, citing a reference made by Mrs. Kennedy, compared the end of the Kennedy administration to the end of Camelot, the mythical kingdom of Great Britain's legendary King Arthur. Within hours of her husband's death, Jackie bravely stood by Vice President Lyndon Johnson as he took the oath of office and assumed the presidency. Later, she personally directed many of the funeral details, and displayed remarkable dignity and composure to a stunned country that shared her grief.

IN HOMAGE
This medal, with the portrait of John F. Kennedy, was designed by noted American artist Paul Manship.

A SOLEMN OATH
In a swift and sad transfer of power, Vice President Lyndon Johnson was sworn in as president shortly after Kennedy's death. The ceremony took place on *Air Force One*, the president's plane. At Johnson's side was a dazed but dignified Mrs. Kennedy, still wearing the pink suit stained with her husband's blood.

Robert F. Kennedy

Jean Kennedy Smith

Peter Lawford

Jacqueline Kennedy

Caroline Kennedy

John F. Kennedy, Jr.

GRIEF AND STRENGTH
Millions of television viewers worldwide watched the president's state funeral. Most were in awe of Jackie's strength as she led her young children down the steps of the U.S. Capitol after the service. Not since the assassination of Abraham Lincoln nearly a hundred years earlier had there been such an outpouring of national grief.

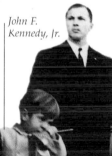

John F. Kennedy, Jr.

Caroline Kennedy Schlossberg

Mrs. Onassis

President Clinton

JACKIE O.
At age forty, Jackie shocked the nation by marrying Greek shipping magnate Aristotle Onassis. The wedding took place on his private island, Skorpios. After his death in 1975, Jackie O., as she was called, embarked on a career in book publishing and was a greatly respected editor.

LEAVING A LEGACY
Jackie established the John Fitzgerald Kennedy Library to commemorate Jack's life. She encouraged her children to play a part in preserving their father's legacy. Here, the family speaks with Bill Clinton, America's forty-second president, at the rededication of the library in 1993.

Lady Bird Johnson

NICKNAMED LADY BIRD, Claudia Taylor grew up in a well-to-do Texas household. Her mother died when Lady Bird was only five, but the shy young girl went on to graduate in the top 10 percent of her college class at the age of twenty. Lady Bird's gracious manner provided the perfect balance to Lyndon Johnson's often harsh and unpredictable behavior. After supporting him through many congressional elections, she campaigned exhaustively for the 1960 Kennedy-Johnson presidential ticket. When Lyndon was sworn in as president after John Kennedy's assassination in 1963, she was at his side.

BEAUTIFYING AMERICA
As first lady, Mrs. Johnson created an awareness of the environment and promoted programs to improve conditions in poverty-stricken neighborhoods. This won her recognition from both Democrats and Republicans.

Model of Lady Bird's campaign train

Campaign button

A POLITICAL DYNAMO
Though occasionally brash, Lyndon was a brilliant politician. Yet his failure to end America's involvement in the Vietnam War lost him his bid for reelection. After one term, he and Lady Bird retired to their ranch in Texas.

Conductor's hat with *Lady Bird Special* patch

LADY BIRD'S SPECIAL
During the 1964 presidential campaign, the first lady made a solo, four-day train trip throughout the south to promote her husband's reelection. The *Lady Bird Special* stopped from Virginia to Louisiana so that Mrs. Johnson could talk to the public about Lyndon's political plans.

American eagle made of gold

AMERICA'S MINERAL HERITAGE
Presented to Lady Bird in 1967, this pin represents America's gem and mineral wealth. The one hundred stones, from all fifty states as well as the District of Columbia, were cut by members of the American Federation of Mineralogical Societies. The brooch itself was designed by Samuel F. Markowitz of New York.

A HEAD START IN LIFE
Mrs. Johnson supported Head Start, a program designed to teach learning skills to underprivileged children, thereby giving them a "head start" in life. In addition to advising and supported her husband on major political issues, she promoted her own causes as well.

Pat Nixon

P<small>AT</small> N<small>IXON</small> <small>LOST BOTH PARENTS</small> by the age of eighteen and valiantly worked her way through college during the Great Depression. Although she disliked politics, during the fifties and sixties she dutifully campaigned for her husband, appealing to women voters by representing the ideals of home and family. When Richard Nixon won his bid for the presidency in 1968, Pat became an energetic goodwill ambassador, traveling around the world on diplomatic missions. She continued the White House renovation started by Jacqueline Kennedy (p. 52), adding more than five hundred antiques and pieces of art. Like some of the first ladies before her, Mrs. Nixon became an unfortunate target during a turbulent period in U.S. history, which saw Americans protest the president's policies on civil rights, women's rights, and the war in Vietnam.

THE FAITHFUL FIRST LADY
Mrs. Nixon stood by her husband in victory and defeat. Here, Pat and Dick share a happy moment at their daughter Tricia's White House wedding in June 1971.

Great Wall of China

Pat paid official visits to eighty-two nations during her term as first lady.

NO MORE WAR!
The Nixon administration was plagued by the Vietnam War, which had not been resolved during Johnson's term. While U.S. soldiers died on foreign soil, protests and demonstrations increased at home. The dove of peace, featured in this button, became a symbol for the antiwar movement.

Nixon was the only president to resign from office, and was later pardoned of any wrongdoing by his successor.

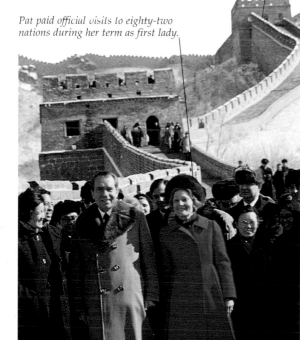

A HISTORIC VISIT
The president and first lady made a historic visit to China in February 1972. Nixon's trip to the Communist country, which had not had diplomatic relations with the United States for decades, helped expand trade and cultural exchanges between the two countries.

A PRESIDENT'S DOWNFALL
Richard Nixon was charged with covering up a break-in at the Democratic Party headquarters in Washington's Watergate complex and resigned in 1974. This is a folk artist's whimsical representation of the Watergate affair.

★ Thelma Catherine Ryan Nixon

PRESIDENT
Richard M. Nixon

YEARS AS FIRST LADY
1969–1974

BORN
March 16, 1912
Ely, Nevada

MARRIED
June 21, 1940
Riverside, California

CHILDREN
Patricia
Julie

DIED
Age 81
June 22, 1993
Park Ridge, New Jersey

Betty Ford

A DIRECT AND LIKABLE FIRST LADY, Betty Ford was not afraid to speak honestly about issues that affected her personal life. Entering the White House suddenly after Richard Nixon's resignation, the former dancer who had raised four children during her husband's rise in politics walked into her first news conference and declared her support of the arts, the elderly, and, most shockingly, the Equal Rights Amendment (ERA)—feminist legislation that her husband strongly opposed. The first lady's frank discussions about her battle with breast cancer, a subject that previously had been avoided in public, inspired many other women to talk about their own experiences with the disease. After Gerry Ford left office, Betty admitted to having a dependence on painkillers and alcohol. She sought professional help and urged others to face their own problems. Later, she founded the now-famous Betty Ford Center for Drug and Alcohol Rehabilitation in Rancho Mirage, California.

READY FOR BETTY
One of Mrs. Ford's aides called her "the most up-front person I ever knew." Although some Americans objected to Betty's outspokenness, most seemed ready for a first lady who believed that "being ladylike does not require silence."

First Mama vest worn by Betty

"10-4 FIRST MAMA"
Betty actively campaigned for her husband in 1976, and was given the affectionate handle First Mama by CB (citizens band) radio users. The public seemed less charmed by Gerry, who lost the election to Jimmy Carter.

Gerald Ford became president without having been elected by the public, the only chief executive to do this.

★

Elizabeth Bloomer Ford

PRESIDENT
Gerald R. Ford

YEARS AS FIRST LADY
1974–1977

BORN
April 8, 1918
Chicago, Illinois

MARRIED
October 15, 1948
Grand Rapids, Michigan

CHILDREN
Michael Gerald
John Gardiner
Steven Meigs
Susan Elizabeth

WASHINGTON STATE WOMEN'S POLITICAL CAUCUS

BETTY, YES! GERRY, NO.

1508- 10th AVE. EAST, SEATTLE, WA. 98102.

Button from
1976 campaign

AN UNELECTED PRESIDENT
When Richard Nixon's vice president, Spiro Agnew, resigned in 1973, Gerald Ford was appointed to succeed him. After Nixon resigned in the wake of the Watergate scandal, Ford became the nation's leader, and tried to restore Americans' confidence in the presidency.

Autographs of Coach George Allen and the Washington Redskins players

GAME BALL
AWARDED TO
MRS. BETTY FORD
FROM COACH GEORGE ALLEN
AND WASHINGTON REDSKINS
WASHINGTON 30 – DENVER 3
SEPTEMBER 30th, 1974
MONDAY NIGHT FOOTBALL

FIRST DOWN, BETTY
The first lady, whose husband had been a star center on the University of Michigan football team, received this game ball while recovering from breast cancer surgery. Mrs. Ford's experience served to educate the public about the disease.

Rosalynn Carter

A SMALL-TOWN GIRL FROM PLAINS, Georgia, Rosalynn Smith was not yet nineteen when she married U.S. Navy midshipman Jimmy Carter. Traveling to six naval bases in seven years opened up an exciting world for the formerly shy honors student. When Jimmy returned to Georgia to take over his father's peanut business, Rosalynn worked alongside him. Later, when he was elected governor of Georgia, she confidently entered the world of politics. During her four years as first lady, Mrs. Carter, as one reporter put it, combined southern charm with a remarkable strength of will. This led some reporters to label her Steel Magnolia.

EXPANDING THE FIRST LADY'S ROLE
As first lady, Mrs. Carter attended cabinet meetings and served as honorary chairperson of the President's Commission on Mental Health. At her husband's request, she also represented him on an official trip to Latin America. During it, she discussed issues and policies with foreign leaders and was, therefore, criticized for exceeding the limits of her position.

A PURSEFUL OF RICHES
King Hassan II of Morocco gave the first lady this gold purse studded with diamonds, rubies, and green onyx.

Jimmy Carter

ADVISER AND ACTIVIST
Rosalynn, seen here with her husband in the Oval Office, was Jimmy's most trusted adviser, and worked hard to bring his concerns to the public. During her first fourteen months as first lady, she visited eighteen foreign nations and twenty-seven U.S. cities, made fifteen major speeches, held twenty-two press conferences, and hosted eighty-three official receptions.

ERA
Mrs. Carter joins hands with former first lady Betty Ford (p. 58) at an Equal Rights Amendment rally. She continued Betty's work to gain the states' support for an amendment to the Constitution guaranteeing equal rights to all regardless of sex.

The hostages were released in January 1981.

THE HOSTAGE CRISIS
In November 1979, militant Iranians took over the U.S. embassy in Tehran and held sixty-six Americans hostage. The captors, followers of the Ayatollah Khomeini, opposed U.S. policy, which refused to officially recognize their leader. Carter's efforts to free the hostages failed and weakened his presidency. The Americans were finally released on his last day in office.

Rosalynn Smith Carter

PRESIDENT
Jimmy Carter

YEARS AS FIRST LADY
1977–1981

BORN
August 18, 1927
Plains, Georgia

MARRIED
July 7, 1946
Plains, Georgia

CHILDREN
John William
James Earl III
Jeffrey
Amy Lynn

Nancy Reagan

Called Queen Nancy by her critics, Nancy Reagan was fiercely protective of her husband and often faulted for having too much power over affairs of state. The child of divorced parents, she grew up in Chicago, Illinois, graduated from Smith College, and became a Hollywood actress. After marrying actor Ronald Reagan in 1952, she retired from the screen to raise their two children while he embarked on a political career. Shortly after entering the White House in 1981, Nancy was met with public disapproval for redecorating the family living quarters, spending large sums on official receptions, and wearing glamorous clothes. Mrs. Reagan countered such attacks with humor, and quickly changed her image to reflect her social concerns.

INAUGURAL ELEGANCE
The first lady's 1981 inaugural gown is made of white lace over silk satin and embroidered with beads. It was designed by James Gallanos of Beverly Hills, California.

JUST SAY NO
Mrs. Reagan adopted drug abuse as her cause and traveled throughout the nation, making appearances to encourage children to "Just Say No" to drugs. In 1985, she hosted a two-day First Ladies Conference on Drug Abuse, which was attended by eighteen wives of world leaders.

THE CHINA SCANDAL
Because Reagan's administration was cutting programs for the poor, Nancy's purchase of a new set of White House china for $200,000 was widely criticized. The public did not realize it was paid for by a private donor, not government funds.

⭐

Nancy Davis Reagan

PRESIDENT
Ronald Reagan

YEARS AS FIRST LADY
1981–1989

BORN
July 6, 1921
New York, New York

MARRIED
March 4, 1952
San Fernando Valley, California

CHILDREN
Patti Davis
Ronald Prescott

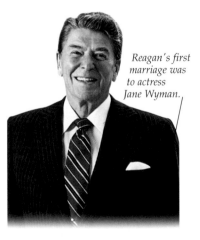

Reagan's first marriage was to actress Jane Wyman.

THE GREAT COMMUNICATOR
A former actor and an extremely popular president, Ronald Reagan was noted for his ease in front of TV cameras. Reagan is the only U.S. president to have been divorced.

Caricature of Ronald Reagan

VOODOO ECONOMICS
A voodoo doll is used to cast spells. This one may be a humorous reference to the president's highly criticized economic policy, which was referred to as "voodoo economics."

Barbara Bush

DUBBED EVERYBODY'S GRANDMOTHER by the press for her unaffected manner and white hair, Barbara Bush devoted her White House years to the cause of literacy. She avoided the controversies that plagued many former first ladies by remaining silent about sensitive political issues that would interfere with her husband's policies and focusing instead on humanitarian concerns. George and Barbara met as teenagers and married during World War II. While George finished school, established an oil business in Texas, and entered politics, Barbara raised their six children. The tragic death of one of their children, Robin, from leukemia instilled in Barbara a compassion for others. Mrs. Bush has written books to support reading programs nationwide as well as a best-selling autobiography.

A LIFE OF SERVICE
George Bush became a congressman in 1966, and later was U.S. ambassador to the United Nations, director of the CIA, and vice president. Barbara's outgoing personality was a great asset to him in his career.

Dan Quayle was Bush's running mate in 1988 and 1992.

BARBARA AND MILLIE
First dog Millie gained celebrity status when Barbara Bush wrote *Millie's Book*, a springer spaniel's view of the White House. Book earnings were donated to the cause of literacy.

STORIES TO GROW ON
Mrs. Bush often visited schools, where she read to children. The first lady organized the Barbara Bush Foundation for Family Literacy—yet still found time to read to her grandchildren.

NO SECOND CHANCE
George won his 1988 campaign for president by promising to create a "kinder and gentler nation." Although he was a strong leader in foreign affairs, he was less successful at grappling with economics and crime. Voters did not reelect him in 1992.

General Norman Schwarzkopf, commander in chief of U.S. forces

George Bush

Barbara Bush

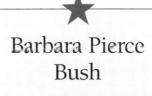

FIRST LADY IN THE FIELD
In 1991, President Bush sent U.S. troops to the Middle East to defend Kuwait, a small nation with valuable oil resources, from its Iraqi invaders. When George visited American soldiers in the war zone, the first lady accompanied him.

Barbara Pierce Bush

PRESIDENT
George Bush

YEARS AS FIRST LADY
1989–1993

BORN
June 8, 1925
Bronx, New York

MARRIED
January 6, 1945
Rye, New York

CHILDREN
George Walker
Robin
John Ellis
Neil Mallon
Marvin Pierce
Dorothy

Hillary Rodham Clinton

EDUCATED IN THE 1960s, a time when women made great strides professionally and politically, Hillary Rodham Clinton was the first presidential spouse who continued her career after marriage—she was a well-established and respected lawyer in Arkansas. With her election to the U.S. Senate in the year 2000, she also became the first one to hold a national office. Hillary had an ambitious view of her role as first lady, and her husband, Bill, shared it, appointing her head of a task force to reform the U.S. health care system.

★

Hillary Rodham Clinton

PRESIDENT
William Jefferson Clinton

YEARS AS FIRST LADY
1993–2001

BORN
October 26, 1947
Park Ridge, Illinois

MARRIED
October 11, 1975
Fayetteville, Arkansas

CHILDREN
Chelsea

A POLITICAL PARTNER
Hillary helped Bill attain his political ambitions, but she suffered personal pain in 1997, when he admitted having an inappropriate relationship with a White House intern.

TAKING OFFICE
On January 20, 1993, the day Bill Clinton was sworn in as president, the Clintons marched down Pennsylvania Avenue in the inaugural parade and then moved into the Executive Mansion with their daughter, Chelsea.

Bill Clinton

A DAZZLING BALL GOWN
Mrs. Clinton wore this violet sheath gown to the 1993 inaugural ball. Designed by Sarah Phillips and made by Barbera Matera, Ltd., the dress is covered with beaded lace and has an organza overskirt.

Beaded lace

Violet sheath

★ ★ ★ ★ ★

CHICAGO WELCOMES HILLARY

★ ★ ★ ★ ★

VOTERS FOR HILLARY
During her husband's 1992 campaign, Hillary won her own following. Bill didn't seem to mind, stating, "I always say, she could be president, too."

HILLARY ON HEALTH CARE
In her effort to create a health care system that would give all Americans affordable and quality health coverage, the first lady talked to hundreds of health care professionals and patients across the country. Ultimately, Congress rejected her plan for reform.

THE SENATOR
On November 7, 2000, Hillary broke the mold for first ladies. Her successful campaign for U.S. senator from New York State received an extraordinary amount of media attention and support, and made history as well.

Laura Bush

A GOOD MATCH
The Bushes have proved to be a good match. Together they weathered the historic presidential election of 2000, which required Supreme Court intervention before George could be declared the winner.

AN ONLY CHILD, LAURA WELCH had a sheltered upbringing in Midland, Texas. Prior to her marriage to George W. Bush, she taught school and earned a degree in library science. When her twin daughters were born in 1981, Laura devoted her time to their care. Although Mrs. Bush has never been an outspoken political partner to her husband, she left her mark on many education and literacy projects when she served as first lady of Texas during George's six years as governor of that state. As first lady, she continues to focus on education and family issues. While quieter in nature than her mother-in-law, former first lady Barbara Bush (p. 61), Laura is an experienced political wife and confidently entered the White House.

> "I never felt I was so traditional. . . . I felt I was in many ways very contemporary."

Laura Bush: Traditional First Lady With a Twist

MAKING HEADLINES
Although Laura Bush was first lady of Texas, the national press was just getting to know her during her husband's run for the presidency. This New York Times headline tried to put her life into perspective for voters.

Button from
2000 campaign

America's Next First Family
George & Laura Bush

RUNNING FOR FIRST LADY
Campaign buttons for George W. Bush featured Laura. The Republicans hoped to appeal to voters by promoting traditional family values. Laura's image as a teacher, librarian, wife, and mother greatly helped their cause.

Laura Bush campaign button

A FAMILY TRADITION
Former first lady Barbara Bush shares a moment with her daughter-in-law, the current first lady. Mrs. Bush is only the second woman in U.S. history to have both a husband and son serve as president. The first was Abigail Adams (p. 8).

★

Laura Welch Bush

PRESIDENT
George W. Bush

YEARS AS FIRST LADY
2001–

BORN
November 4, 1946
Midland, Texas

MARRIED
November 5, 1977
Midland, Texas

CHILDREN
Barbara
Jenna

Index

Acknowledgments

The author and Dorling Kindersley offer their grateful thanks to:
Edith P. Mayo, curator emeritus at the Smithsonian's National Museum of American History; Ellen Nanney of the Smithsonian's Office of Product Development and Licensing; Kate Henderson of the Smithsonian's National Museum of American History; Heather Egan and Beverly Cox of the Smithsonian's National Portrait Gallery; Jim Bruns and James O'Donnell of the Smithsonian's National Postal Museum; Robert Johnston of the Smithsonian American Art Museum; the following curators, archivists, and photography professionals from both presidential libraries and private institutions: James Hill, Don Holloway, Mark Renovitch, Michelle Frauenberger, Anthony Guzzi, Mindy Haines, Isabel Parker, Harmony Haskins, Marion Kamm, Maureen Harding, Jennifer Pedersen, Susan Naulty, Debbie Bush, Kathy Tabb, David Stanhope, Victoria Kalemaris, Thomas Price, Kay Tyler, David Smolen, Kelly Fearnow, Allison Enos, Kelly Cobble, Hanna Edwards, Peggy Flynn, and Bettina Demetz; and especially Oliver, Nicholas, and Peter Pastan. Dianne Carroll provided additional photography.

Photography Credits
(t = top; b = bottom; l = left; r = right;
c = center; a = above)

AP/World Wide Photos: 50lb. Archive Photos: 55lb Express Newspapers, 55br Gary Cameron. Bold Concepts: 63c. George Bush Presidential Library: 61tl, 61lc, 61b. Jimmy Carter Library: 59lc, 59lb, 59rc. Corbis: 7t Todd Gipstein, 47t, 52l, 63tl, 63b. Chicago Historical Society: 27b. George Eastman House: 38rb. Dwight D. Eisenhower Library: 51lb, 51rc, 51ra. Gerald R. Ford Presidential Museum: 58lc, 58rb Dianne Carroll. Rutherford B. Hayes Presidential Center: 28rb, 29c. The Hermitage, Home of President Andrew Jackson, Nashville, TN: 16tl, 16c, 16cb, 16r. Herbert Hoover Library: 44ca, 45tl, 45lb. Andrew Johnson National Historical Site, Greeneville, TN: 26rb. John F. Kennedy Library: 52r, 53tl, 53ca, 53b, 53r, 54tl, 55tr, 55c. Library of Congress: 14lc, 17t, 17lb, 18tl, 18cb, 22l, 23b, 23lb, 26l, 30tl, 31tl, 35tl, 37bl, 37b, 38tl, 42l, 43rb, 50tl, 51tl. Mary Todd Lincoln House: 22c. James Madison's Montpelier, Orange, VA: 13lb, 13cb. Monticello/Thomas Jefferson Memorial Foundation, Inc.: 10–11b, 11tl, 11lc, 11c, 11tr. Mount Vernon Ladies' Association:

5rc, 5rb, 6c, 7lb, 7c. National Archives and Records Administration: 47ca. National Museum of American Art, Smithsonian Institution: 5lb, 15tl, 16c, 21lc, 21lb, 57c. National Museum of American History: 4c, 5tr, 6tl, 6tr, 6rc, 9tr, 13rc, 15c, 17ca, 17rb, 18c, 19c, 19rc, 20tl, 20la, 23tl, 23c, 24tr, 25c, 25lb, 26r, 27rc, 30bl, 32b, 32tr, 33tl, 33lc, 33lb, 33c, 33r, 35c, 37ra, 39la, 42b, 42c, 42cr, 43c, 43ra, 44cb, 45la, 47l, 47c, 50rb, 51rb, 54bl, 60c, 60rb, 62c, 62r. National Portrait Gallery: 4l, 5lc, 6b, 7b, 8tr, 10tl, 12lb, 13tl, 13rb, 14rc, 15lb, 17ca, 17cb, 18rb, 19lb, 20lc, 20rb, 20ca, 21rb, 22tr, 25tr, 26ca, 27tl, 27tr, 29c, 31c, 34c, 38bl, 39tr, 42tr, 43lb, 44lb, 47rb, 48tl Ruth Orkin, 50ca, 51ca, 56ra, 59tl, 60bl. National Postal Museum: 45r, 49rc. New Hampshire Historical Society: 20tl, 20rc. *New York Times*: 56tl George Tames, 63ca. Richard Nixon Library and Birthplace: 57tl, 57lb. James K. Polk Memorial Association, Columbia, TN: 19tl, 19rb. Ronald Reagan Library: 60tl. Franklin D. Roosevelt Library: 46c, 48tc, 48br, 49bl, 49tr. Sagamore Hill National Historic Site: 36lb, 36cb. Sherwood Forest Plantation: 18lc. Smithsonian Institution: 9la, 10c, 10b, 12ra, 13c, 14la, 14cb, 16lb, 17ra, 20rc, 20lb, 24tl, 24rb, 25lc, 27lc, 27ca, 29tl, 29bl, 29c, 29r, 30c,

30rb, 31bl, 31br, 32tl, 34bl, 34bc, 34r, 35lb, 35c, 35r, 36ca, 36tr, 37tl, 37lc, 38c, 38ra, 39ca, 39lb, 39rb, 40tl, 40tr, 40b, 41l, 41tr, 41c, 41br, 43tl, 44tl, 47r, 48la, 50ra, 54bl, 54tr, 55tl, 56l, 56cb, 56rb, 57lc, 58c, 58r, 59rb, 61tr, 61r. Sophia Smith Collection, Smith College: 24lc. United States Department of the Interior, National Park Service, Adams National Historical Park: 8l, 8rc, 8b, 9c, 15tr. University of New Hampshire Media Center: 46l Trude Fleischmann. The White House: 58tl, 62tl, 62lc, 62lb. White House Collection, Courtesy White House Historical Association: 9b, 12tl, 12rb, 18lb, 28l, 36tl, 60ca.

Jacket Credits
Dwight D. Eisenhower Library: tl, back rb. Gerald R. Ford Presidential Museum: back rc. Library of Congress: back lc. National Museum of American History: tl, tr, front ca, front ra, front lc, front rc, front cb, back la, back rc, back ra, spine. National Portrait Gallery: back lb. National Postal Museum: front la. Smithsonian Institution: tcl, tc, tcr, front bl, front rb, back cb.